CORPORATE CONFIDENTIAL

WHAT IT REALLY TAKES
TO GET TO THE TOP

Susan A. DePhillips

**PLATINUM
PRESS™**

AVON, MASSACHUSETTS

Published by
Platinum Press™, an imprint of Adams Media,
an F+W Publications Company
57 Littlefield Street, Avon, MA 02322. U.S.A.
www.adamsmedia.com

Platinum Press™ is a trademark of F+W Publications, Inc.

ISBN: 1-59337-349-X

Printed in the United States of America.

J I H G F E D C B A

Library of Congress Cataloging-in-Publication Data
DePhillips, Susan A.
Corporate confidential / Susan A. DePhillips.
p.   cm.
ISBN 1-59337-349-X
1. Success in business. 2. Organizational behavior.
3. Executives—Psychology. I. Title.
HF5386.D43 2005
650.1—dc22
2005002134

This publication is designed to provide accurate and authoritative information with
regard to the subject matter covered. It is sold with the understanding that the pub-
lisher is not engaged in rendering legal, accounting, or other professional advice. If
legal advice or other expert assistance is required, the services of a competent professional person should be sought.

—From a *Declaration of Principles* jointly adopted by a
Committee of the American Bar Association and a
Committee of Publishers and Associations

Many of the designations used by manufacturers and sellers to distinguish their product are claimed as trademarks. Where those designations appear in this book and
Adams Media was aware of a trademark claim, the designations have been printed
with initial capital letters.

This book is available at quantity discounts for bulk purchases.
For information, please call 1-800-872-5627.

Dedication

I dedicate this book to my beloved father, Anthony J. DePhillips, who taught me the value of hard work and served as a constant role model of integrity and self-sacrifice. I love you, Dad.

In loving memory of my mother, the late Mary Lucile DePhillips, who believed that every woman should have an informed opinion and who instilled in me the confidence and courage to believe that anything is possible in a lifetime. Your guidance and presence are still felt.

CONTENTS

Acknowledgments

I would like to express my deepest gratitude to each executive who so graciously gave of his or her time and candor to this book. I would also like to express my sincerest appreciation to my agent, Frank Weimann, for working so diligently on my behalf; and to Adams Media, and my editor, Jill Alexander, for taking a chance on a first-time author.

To my mentors, Susan and Stephen Joyce: my deepest affection for your guidance and support throughout my corporate career. Many thanks to my dearest friends: Ivy, for your guidance and unwavering support; Krista, for teaching me about the realities of the publishing world; Ezra, for keeping me grounded when I was losing perspective on the project; Rick and Will, for always offering me a safe haven; Tom and Laura, for helping me keep my sense of humor throughout this process; and Stephanie, for always lending me an ear when I needed one.

To Peter, thank you for your constant support, love, and willingness to put yourself second behind my work. I am truly blessed to have you in my life.

orporate success. Everyone wants it, but few truly know the secrets to achieving it. Ask any professional to describe his or her biggest frustration with work, and inevitably you will hear, "I thought I'd be further along in my career," or, "I'm not being recognized the way I should be." Implicit in both responses is the belief that achievement of career goals is beyond one's control. Essentially, many professionals know what they want; what they often don't know is how to achieve it.

In today's climate of economic uncertainty coupled with escalating unemployment, you need every bit of leverage you can obtain to improve your career standing and potential. The harsh reality is that if you're not constantly moving forward, you're losing professional ground—and more aggressive colleagues won't hesitate to poach your position, projects, and opportunities. As a former vice president of human resources with twenty years of corporate experience,

I have counseled hundreds of professionals on performance improvement issues and coached them on how to develop promotional strategies within an organization. Pick up one of the myriad of books written about corporate "effectiveness" or "success," and all too often you find consultants and academics touting intellectual theories and perpetuating useless jargon. These approaches typically serve only to perpetuate cookie-cutter behavior in the corporate world. As a result, I decided to write a book detailing the specific actions that could immediately be applied in the workplace.

In *Corporate Confidential,* I have incorporated my own professional experience and opinions on achieving corporate success with findings from candid, one-on-one interviews with senior *Fortune* 500 executives representing a variety of disciplines and industries. My hope is that this book provides simple and straightforward answers about what it takes to achieve success in the corporate world. It addresses some of the important lessons we've learned and provides an honest, though not always comfortable, perspective on success and failure in corporate America. These truths, usually unspoken, are expressed by people who have worked for the largest corporations and achieved the highest levels of success.

In short, *Corporate Confidential* is a most insightful book about what it really takes to get to the top of the nation's most successful organizations.

1 | THE CAST OF CHARACTERS

When I began my journey of researching this book, I was cautiously optimistic that I could secure enough key *Fortune* 500 executives who would be willing to share inside information about what it takes to be successful in the corporate world. Having devoted almost twenty years to my own corporate career, I also realized that it would be challenging to have these executives agree to make their identities public.

I spent hundreds of hours working with various public affairs departments, with the promise that no quotations would be attributed to any particular executive. I clearly underestimated the corporate reticence, displayed all too often when company representatives were asked for honest insights into the politics and nuances of the corporate world. On average, only one of every ten executives I contacted agreed to contribute to the book. Those who did participate were enthusiastic about telling the truth about their own experiences and challenge of maneuvering through corporate America.

Each of these interviews lasted approximately two hours and was conducted either face-to-face or over the phone. Flexibility was the key in securing these interviews, as these executives are indeed busy people. While conducting interviews in New York, I received a last-minute phone call from one executive who asked if I might meet him at the train station in Washington, D.C., at least two hours by train from Manhattan. He was very apologetic about the change and explained that he had been called to a meeting at the White House. In another instance, I had to conduct the phone interview in two parts, as the executive could only talk from the car during his commute home.

I was able to interview some executives in their offices, and it was quite an experience to visit a variety of corporate campuses scattered across the United States. As I arrived at each location, I was taken aback by the different cultures. In one instance, I drove up a long, winding private road guarded by hundreds of tall spruce trees. Off in the distance, I could see several elaborate mansions that, as I later learned, housed many of the company's executives. In another facility, I arrived at a cluster of buildings that looked like something out of a science fiction movie.

The other interesting thing about these visits was the treatment I received once the receptionist learned I was headed to the executive floor. Indirect exposure to these executives somehow gave me instant respect with the support staff, and I was treated as a VIP. While on the one hand this was flattering, their behavior also made me more conscious of the preconceived notions that so many staffers harbor about the executive wing and those who are housed there.

Once I gained access to those top floors, I understood how corporate culture perpetuates many of those perceptions. In some instances, I was struck by the old-school, ultra-traditional aura of some companies. I remember walking down the long, wood-floored corridor of one executive wing, lined with painted portraits of the company's stoic founding fathers, being ever so cautious not to speak too loudly. In other companies, however, the executive floors were bubbling with conversation and laughter. Some corporations maintained a very traditional corporate dress code while others were swarming with professionals in khakis and golf shirts.

Many of the executive offices were larger than most people's living rooms and full of accoutrements. During one interview, I remember being distracted by a constant stream of ticker symbols and stock prices on the multiple television screens. In yet another, my eye caught a series of photos of the executive posing with several U.S. presidents and other high-ranking officials.

Regardless of their trappings, all the executives I interviewed were gracious, open, and easy to talk to—even about the most sensitive issues. It was as if they had been waiting for someone to ask them what they really thought about the corporate world. I was happy to oblige. I should also mention that while I offered to pay each executive a stipend—after all, they were giving several hours of their time—they all refused any compensation for their participation.

General Demographic Information About the Executives

The executives interviewed for this book can be broken down into demographic categories as follows:

SEX
Male: 75%
Female: 25%

AGE
60 to 70: 10%
50 to 59: 54%
40 to 49: 30%
30 to 39: 6%

ETHNICITY
Caucasian: 90%
African American: 4.5%
Hispanic: 4.5%

HIGHEST DEGREE OF EDUCATION
High school diploma: 7%
Bachelor's degree: 45%
Advanced degree: 48%

MARITAL STATUS
Married: 93%
Single/divorced: 7%

Even at first glance, you can see the wide range of generations represented in the executive ranks of the corporate world, along with a variety of educational backgrounds. The majority of this successful cadre is still Caucasian, though I was happy to see an increase in the number of minority professionals who had attained such commanding positions in the corporate world.

While this demographic information provides only a statistical snapshot of the participating executives, the correlation and significance of this information as it relates to corporate success is discussed throughout the book. In addition, I share further insight into the executives' various backgrounds and patterns of upbringing that often influenced their career choices and overall success.

The *Fortune* 500 Executives Interviewed for This Book

In targeting the specific *Fortune* 500 executives to interview for this book, I consciously sought out a cross-section of professionals across geographic areas, industries, and specific disciplines of responsibility. I strived to create a balance of male and female executives.

The following executives permitted me to include their names as contributors:

Guy P. Abramo
Executive Vice President
Chief Strategy and Information
 Officer
Ingram Micro, Inc.

Arnold A. Allemang
Executive Vice President,
 Operations
The Dow Chemical Company

Arthur B. Anderson
Senior Vice President (former)
Advanced Technology
PepsiCo, Inc.

John D. Austin
Senior Vice President
Chief Financial Officer
Performance Food Group

Mary Beth Bardin
Executive Vice President (former)
Public Affairs & Communication
Verizon

Patricia J. Brown
Vice President
Global Branding and
    Communications
Cooper Tire & Rubber Company

Catherine S. Brune
Senior Vice President
Chief Technology Officer
Allstate Insurance Company

Dick DiCerchio
Senior Executive Vice President
Chief Operating Officer
Costco Wholesale

Patricia Engels
Executive Vice President (former)
Qwest

Richard H. Glanton
Senior Vice President
Mergers & Acquisitions
Exelon Corporation

Patrick J. Gnazzo
Vice President
Business Practices
United Technologies Corporation

Greg Greene
Senior Vice President
Strategic Planning & Development
Ryder System, Inc.

Robert A. Hagemann
Senior Vice President
Chief Financial Officer
Quest Diagnostics, Inc.

Steven Hankins
Chief Financial Officer
Tyson Foods, Inc.

Rojon D. Hasker
Senior Vice President
Marketing & Merchandising
Safeway Stores, Inc.

JoAnn Heffernan Heisen
Executive Committee
Vice President
Chief Information Officer
Johnson & Johnson

Carlos M. Hernandez
General Counsel & Secretary
International Steel Group, Inc.
(Former Executive Vice
        President, General Counsel
        & Secretary—Fleming
        Companies, Inc.)

Andrew Herring
Executive Vice President
Supervalu Retail Pharmacies

Michael P. Huseby
Executive Vice President
Chief Financial Officer
Cablevision Systems Corporation

Joshua R. Jewett
Senior Vice President
Chief Information Officer
Family Dollar Stores, Inc.

David Kornblatt
Vice President
Chief Financial Officer
York International Corporation

Paula Kruger
Executive Vice President
President, Consumer Markets
        Group
Qwest

Cathy L. Lewis
Senior Vice President
Marketing
IKON Office Solutions

Keith W. Lovett
Senior Vice President (retired)
Human Resources
Rite Aid Corporation

Steve Lowden
Senior Vice President
Business Development and
        Integrated Gas
Marathon Oil Corporation

John W. Marsland
Vice President
Corporate Development Office
Air Products and Chemicals, Inc.

Chuck McCaig
Chief Information Officer
Chubb Corporation

Diane McGarry
Vice President
Chief Marketing Officer
Xerox Corporation

Rosanne O'Brien
Corporate Vice President
Communications
Northrop Grumman Corporation

William G. Pagonis
Head of Supply Chain
President, Sears Logistics Services,
    Inc.
Sears, Roebuck and Company

Steve Parrish
Senior Vice President
Corporate Affairs
Altria Group, Inc.

Erik R. Pekarski
National Vice President
Customer Relations
Pulte Homes, Inc.

Bob Prieto
Senior Vice President
Fluor Corporation
(Former Chairman of Parsons
    Brinckerhoff, Inc.)

Robert R. Ridout
Vice President
Chief Information Officer
DuPont Company

Dennis E. Ross
Vice President
General Counsel
Ford Motor Company

Richard W. Severance
Senior Vice President (retired)
Downstream Strategy,
    Optimization & Business
    Development
ConocoPhillips

Darryl G. Smette
Senior Vice President
Marketing & Midstream
Devon Energy Corporation

Robert S. Stewart
Senior Vice President
Centex Corporation

Connie Weaver
Executive Vice President
Public Relations, Marketing &
    Brand
AT&T

Mark (Denny) Weinberg
President & CEO
Arcus Industries, Inc.
(A wholly owned subsidiary of
    Wellpoint Health Networks,
    Inc.)

Charles E. Williams
Senior Vice President
Operations
Waste Management, Inc.

Carl Wilson
Executive Vice President
Chief Information Officer
Marriott International, Inc.

Kenneth A. Wolinsky
Vice President
Chief Information Officer
Avery Dennison Corporation

Other *Fortune* 500 executives were interviewed for this book, but they were either uncomfortable about or specifically prohibited by their organizations from being cited as a contributor. Though these executives can't be credited, their insights and examples are included with those listed above.

Born into Affluence?

During these interviews, I was most surprised by the candor of these executives regarding their own upbringing, career decisions, motivations, and experiences in the corporate world. They revealed their feelings about reaching the executive level; about the misconceptions that too many professionals harbor about them; about their motivation to continue working in such a demanding world—even after they've achieved both positional and financial success; and about the sacrifices and trade-offs they made along the way.

The most insightful part of the interviews was learning about the childhood and upbringing of these professionals. One might think that the majority of these power players were born into affluence, and somehow had a "leg up" on the rest of the world. That is a misconception that couldn't be further from the truth. With the exception of one or two individuals I interviewed, most of the executives came from meager and humble beginnings. Most grew up in the blue-collar world, with families doing work that ranged from sharecropping to day labor. During their adolescence, they often moved several times as a result of their father's work. In several cases, these professionals lost their father at a very young age and, as a result, were either raised by grandparents or a single mother.

One common thread that bound virtually all of these executives was that each individual started working, typically out of necessity, at a very young age. As youngsters they worked in jobs ranging from farmhands to construction workers. Some worked in a variety of roles in the family business. In one instance, a female executive was buying goods in New York's garment district at the age of sixteen.

What was even more remarkable was that, despite the challenging conditions some of these individuals experienced in their childhood and early adult years, none of them expressed regret. All these executives proudly told me the story of their parents and the environment in which they grew up. Each could articulate the correlation of their upbringing to their attitude, work ethic, and ultimately to their level of professional success in the corporate world. All had struggled, suffered great losses, fallen down, and even failed along the way, but they still managed to reach the top. What made these individuals unusual was not the advantages they had been given but their unyielding tenacity when it came to overcoming obstacles in their path.

While visiting these senior executives, I observed their interactions with both colleagues and subordinates and overheard many telephone conversations. Interestingly enough, I found the majority of them not only courteous but also very down to earth in their dealings with people at all levels in the organization. As I learned of their life experiences, I knew their personal style was no coincidence. From their early work experiences and exposure to many different types of people in the world, most recognized that no one person is better than another. As one executive simply put it, "People are people." Another executive shared this comment about the preconceived ideas of many corporate executives: "Some executives think that if you get to know all levels of employees then you potentially have to give them something . . . or they (the employees) will take something from you. Some executives need to remember where they came from." Each executive spoke with such respect and admiration about his or her organization and its employees that it was easy for me to see why they had achieved such senior levels in the corporation.

How These Executives View Their Careers

Virtually every person interviewed used the adjective "fun" in describing their perspective about work. One executive shared this insight: "It used to mystify me that people who made so much money still continued to work. Until I figured it out—they actually love it! It's a game!" Another executive advised young professionals not to make the same mistake he did: "I wish I knew earlier on in my career just how fun it is to have a lot of responsibility . . . I fought everything and in the beginning, took it all too seriously." That is not to say that the executives didn't also describe their jobs as "pressure cookers" and oftentimes as exhausting and frustrating. Overall, however, they genuinely love what they do in the corporate world. In fact, several executives reinforced the importance of choosing a career that one has passion for and will enjoy performing day in and day out. As one executive said, "Corporate America is demanding. If you're going to devote most of your life to your career, you sure as hell better enjoy it!"

For many of these power players, another personal motivation to achieve senior levels within an organization stemmed from an innate desire to directly influence the success (or failure) of a corporation. In some instances the executives defined "influence" in the context of functioning as a true "change agent." As one executive commented, "I'm a real believer that the only way to make change is be part of it." Several other executives, however, described professional influence as a means of controlling their own destiny in the corporate world. One executive explained it best: "Throughout so much of one's career you don't have control—decisions get passed down that you weren't involved with and yet you have to make it palatable to people . . . at some point in my career I came to the realization that if I could sit at the top of the company, there would be no more of the passing it down. I could stop playing the messenger!"

Driven by Success?

Many readers of this book may think that any executive's reply to the question, "Are you driven by a desire to succeed?" would be a simple "Of course!" Interestingly enough, however, the answer given by most executives was far more complex. Most female executives, for instance, tended to be far more definitive about their desire to succeed than their male counterparts. In fact, when asked whether they feared failure, most female executives commented that they never considered failure as an option. A few of the women even responded to the question in a manner that left me with the impression that they see fear-driven behavior as a character flaw. As one female executive put it, "Oh, I see it all the time; men, and the power they exert, is driven by a fear of failure."

Among the male executives, however, there tended to be some degree of overlap between the desire to succeed and the desire to avoid failure in the job. At least half of the men interviewed went on to say that even as they achieved senior-level positions, there was an overriding motivation not to disappoint those individuals who had entrusted them with these critical jobs. In a few instances, male executives shared their further fear that eventually they would be "found out" by their superiors as somehow having fooled everyone about their actual capabilities. As one executive expressed, "It's the fear of being tap water and not Perrier." This perspective resonated with several other executives, who also experienced the same anxiety. While we can only speculate on the psychology of that fear, it is reasonable to surmise that in regard to the motivation of highly driven individuals, there is a fine line between seeking success and a fear of failure.

A number of executives (especially the female executives) spoke about the conscious thought of success as a means of sustaining a livelihood. As one executive put it, "Once you've grown up on the other side of the tracks, it's not that far to fall back . . . so there is always that fear for me." Such a remark was not surprising considering the modest or underprivileged upbringing of many of the executives interviewed.

EXECUTIVE SUMMARY

While it was clear that most of the executives are indeed incredibly committed to their success and the success of their respective corporations, I also sensed a "kinder and gentler" approach in the methods of these corporate powerhouses. As one executive commented, "Early on, I learned from many corporate leaders what not to do. I remember thinking to myself that I will never berate the heck out of people, embarrass professionals in front of other people, or call them names that simply shouldn't be used." At a time when most of the executives receiving media attention are those demonstrating greedy and unethical behaviors, it was refreshing to spend time with successful executives who were genuinely driven to contribute to their respective organizations in a significant way. Though those interviewed certainly appreciated the financial rewards and perks that accompanied their positions, the majority of them were far more motivated and excited by the "means" rather than the "end." ◉

2 | WITH SUCCESS COMES SACRIFICE

For all too many professionals, the desire to achieve an executive position often overshadows any understanding of the true realities and concessions required to attain such levels in an organization. In virtually every interview I conducted, each executive detailed the trade-offs made for the sake of their career. I deliberately use the word "trade-off," rather than "sacrifice," because most executives believe that the compromises made were clearly worth the long-term rewards. That is not to say that these corporate officers are without regret about the choices they might have made along the way. Overall, however, most would not change any of their decisions. In fact, most of the executives reinforced the importance of not looking back at the choices made over the course of their careers. As one executive shared, "You can't turn the clock back, so why devote time to agonizing over choices that have already been made?"

When you consider that approximately 90 percent of this cadre are over forty years of age, you begin to understand that these professionals grew up in corporate America at a time when "paying one's dues" was the credo of most large corporations. In fact, each executive attributed his or her success, at least in part, to an ability to work hard. I share this information because it is important for anyone who wants to get ahead in today's corporate environment to understand the background and professional upbringing of this "management generation." The individuals represented in this book directly influence the rewards and promotional opportunities that are extended or withheld in corporate America.

The members of this executive class fully acknowledge the difficult choices that they as professionals have had to make during their careers. At the same time, they absolutely affirm the belief that to achieve great success in the corporate world, one is required to devote tremendous time and effort and to sacrifice personal objectives along the way.

For any who think that once they achieve an executive-level position, the demands of the job will somehow diminish, think again. These senior executives consistently work an average of sixty-five hours per week, and that number does not reflect the time they spend working outside the office. As one executive expressed it, "The time commitment is enormous. You're always on the job even when you're at home." In fact, most executives further commented on their belief that the majority of working people are under the misconception that executive-level jobs are somehow easier than most positions in a corporation. As one executive put it, "People underestimate the constant pressure there is at this level . . . we're up plenty of nights thinking and worrying. Most [people] see it as flying around in the corporate jet and getting paid enormous amounts of money." Another executive made the comment that "Too many [people] view my job as simply sitting behind a desk, telling other people what to do."

These senior folks may not expect staff members to fully appreciate the demands of their jobs, but they do want other professionals to understand the tremendous pressure and risk associated with these executive-level positions. If an individual wants to hold such a rank in an organization, it is imperative for him or her to understand that there is more to the title than money and stock options. The title also comes with intense pressure and a tremendous amount of actual work that must be accomplished.

Gaining insight into the demands placed on the time of these executives might lead you to believe that they expect their staff to spend the same number of hours with nose to the grindstone. I was surprised by the executives' perspective on this issue. When asked about how they correlate hours worked to overall performance, the majority of these executives stated that they care more about the results their employees achieve than the number of hours they put in on the job. In fact, at least half of the group suggested that when an employee is working an exorbitant amount of hours, it is indicative of ineffective performance, a disorganized employee with no time-management skills, or a flaw in the design of the position. One executive shared this perspective: "Some of the most unproductive people work the most hours."

That being said, however, many of the executives also reinforced that their exceptional performers tend to produce greater results and work longer hours than those employees deemed as "average." Most of the executives believe that the high achievers, and those professionals who attain the promotions, are not those working a traditional forty-hour workweek. In fact, most of the executives believe that there is no such thing as a "traditional" workweek. As one executive commented, "I've never met a successful person who says they work nine to five."

On the one hand, these influential folks absolutely acknowledge the time investment that highly driven people must commit to work. At the same time, as managers of these people, the executives had a genuine desire to give them more of a personal life than they might have experienced during their own climb up the corporate ladder. They admit, however, that this mindset is a significant departure from the "old school" management style of previous decades.

Visibility Counts

While these executives strive to provide greater flexibility to their employees, virtually all of them commented that the issue of "face time" still exists in the corporate world. The behavior of face time, as I defined it for the executives, is best described as being the first one in to the office in the morning or the last one to leave at night in an attempt to gain the boss's favor. The executives stated that while they continue to observe that behavior, it is practiced to a far lesser degree than it was, say, ten years ago. To what degree this practice is being phased out, however, is hard to gauge and of course will vary from corporation to corporation.

One executive cited a recent example involving the new chief executive officer (CEO) of his company. When this CEO started work at the organization, he typically arrived at his office around seven-thirty in the morning. This executive began to notice that much of the office also began to arrive at seven-thirty. Coincidence? No way. The executive was taken aback by the immature behavior of his peers, as it was reminiscent of the days when CEOs walked the halls taking a mental roll call. Interestingly enough, however, one afternoon the CEO peered in to this executive's office and said, "So, you left early yesterday?" This executive found himself defensively explaining that he actually had a late meeting in another building. As the executive sarcastically commented, "You'd think at this level it wouldn't matter, but it still does."

When all was said and done, it became abundantly clear that an interesting dichotomy exists today in the corporate world. On the one hand, these senior-level jobs place tremendous demands on the executives, yet this group still strives to provide greater accommodation to their own employees. This contradiction is perhaps best illustrated in the following quote from one executive: "I am flexible to a degree regarding work schedules and time off. I encourage my folks to plan vacations, and I do not call them during that time off. I do need them to be flexible with their schedules around key business events like earnings releases or period closings. That attitude, however, is not the norm for me. I can be called any time, twenty-four hours a day, and am not always given the same consideration I try to give my people."

The bottom line is that highly driven professionals need to understand the contradiction involving hours worked and performance that exists in the corporate world, but they should focus on correlating their time and effort to producing tangible and measurable results. These executives are living proof that the greater path to success is by delivering performance rather than worrying about showing their bosses how many hours they have worked.

The Price of Success

Little did Sir Isaac Newton realize as he drafted his laws of physics that these natural principles would also have application in the corporate world. It is true that for every action a driven professional makes along an executive career path, there is also an equal and opposite reaction on the personal side of the equation. As the executives describe, these trade-offs involve three primary areas of life:

Family—Career demands have had an impact on marriage, children, and the overall time available to these professionals to devote to the family unit.

Personal time—Time invested in career pursuits means less time available for personal interests, hobbies, social activities, and cultivating friendships.

Health—Maintaining such a demanding professional pace means there is less time for physical activity—this takes its toll, both physically and mentally.

Again, it is important to note that these executives can clearly articulate the personal trade-offs resulting from career demands. Beyond that, most of these successful folks view these concessions as reasonable. The "collateral damage" to family, personal time, and health is seen as an even exchange for securing an executive-level position and acquiring tremendous responsibility in a corporation.

Family

As it relates to family, time spent at work has an adverse impact on relationships with both spouses and children. The majority of executives commented on periods of great strain on their marriage; some experienced marriages that broke up, at least in part, as a result of the demands of the job. As one executive shared, "My first two marriages failed as a result of my career and ambition . . . having too much on my plate and being virtually gone for years on end." Approximately 30 percent of the executives interviewed talked about compromises their spouses had made, whether in terms of either putting their own careers on hold or giving them up altogether.

The most sensitive of issues, and the one area in which executives actually talked about having some regret, involved their relationships with their children. As one executive put it, "There was a chunk of time that I was just gone, both figuratively and literally, when my daughter was a young teen. I missed that part of her life." Another is more explicit about what was traded for professional success: "I regret that there were periods of my kids' childhood that I don't even remember. They will tell stories about special events or little tragedies that they recall and I think, where was I?"

In discussing the issue of managing a balance in life between family and work, executives reinforced the importance of making choices. Throughout their careers, each executive had to make conscious choices about where their time was best spent. In most cases, the choice was to devote the majority of time to work. This was particularly true when the choice was between the demands of the career and the day-to-day concerns of the family. Some executives did consistently commit time to family events they considered important. For example, one never missed his son's Little League games, while another made certain that his family took a two-week vacation together every year. Several of the executives advise professionals to be realistic about the demands of both career and family. One female executive provided this counsel: "Know the demands of your career and be prepared to meet those expectations. Schedule your personal and family obligations around those demands to the degree that you can . . . let your boss know what family commitments you simply have to give priority to so that both of you can be upfront about professional and personal needs."

For some executives, professional careers were marked by a period in which family crises made it necessary to make dramatic changes at work. One example involved an executive whose wife suffered from clinical depression. He found himself in a difficult situation, not only having to share a very personal problem with his boss, but then having to ask for accommodations in his work schedule. In other cases, the modification to the professional's work life resulted from significant problems with teenage children that required immediate intervention. The interesting insight I gained from these extreme cases was that there was no hesitation on the part of the executives to drastically change their work habits for the sake of the family interest. In discussing these personal matters, what did remain unclear was whether the executives attributed the problems that family member had experienced to themselves and their careers. Without directly admitting it, many did eventually convey that, to some extent, they do feel they are to blame. Again, such guilt, coupled with the genuine concern for the family member, spoke to personal sacrifices many of these executives have made for the sake of their organizations and their careers.

Striving for Balance Between Life and Work

As we talked about the issue of making time for both family and work, I asked the executives for their opinions on corporate initiatives involving alternative work schedules for employees. More than half of the group spoke passionately about these structured programs. While some executives believe that there is a valid purpose for providing alternative work schedules in the business world, most believe that these programs do more harm than good.

Specifically, they believe that while corporations may genuinely be interested in accommodating the needs of their employees, the by-product of these programs is that corporations send mixed messages to professionals, particularly those who are younger, about the balance between family and work life. For example, offering alternative work schedules such as compressed workweeks or telecommuting conveys the message that a professional can take advantage of these flexible work structures and still achieve senior-level status. Essentially, the corporate message is that professionals can have it all.

The majority of executives interviewed vehemently disagreed with this implication. One executive put it this way: "Alternative work schedules set up unrealistic expectations with most working people and for the younger ones . . . they can't appreciate the consequences of these types of programs."

So why then do corporations offer such programs? According to a number of the executives, alternative work schedules are offered as an added benefit to the "average" working population, which represents approximately 75 percent of the organization. The interesting contradiction, however, is that the majority of executives confessed that they are far *less* likely to provide concessions to the average staff member and far *more* willing to make accommodations to their top performers. As one executive remarked, "If an employee wants me to make a concession, they better make it worthwhile. If that employee is giving me all the right information and has demonstrated their value to the company, I'd probably go for it. If, on the other hand, the person is a middle-of-the-road player, then I'm not going for it." Another executive shared this opinion: "I guess the way I look at it is that we've had employees who wanted to go to flextime and when it's a super performer and it doesn't hurt their career, I am more willing to accommodate them because I don't want to lose them."

Several of the executives, however, candidly remarked that these modified schedules often serve as yet another public relations ploy for certain corporations. One executive stated in reference to such programs that "It's a corporate veil." Several executives shared their belief that too often corporations are quick to throw money at a corporate culture issue. The business implements "stuff" to demonstrate its responsiveness to employee concerns without thinking through the clear objectives for offering such programs. One executive shared the following example. His company had conducted an employee survey, and the culture received very low scores on work/life balance. As he remarked, "The company quickly instituted a whole bunch of programs to show their employees that they cared about work/life balance: on-site child care, dry cleaning service, even pet insurance . . . modified work schedules were just another part of the program."

Many corporations and even some executives accommodate flexible work schedules for select professionals. But the truth of the matter, according to most of the executives interviewed, is that a professional can't have it all. While many admit that flexible schedules in some jobs might not be as detrimental to a professional's career, most key professional roles require consistent engagement in the corporation, every single day. As one executive put it, "Corporate jobs dictate a significant commitment. It might not be fair, but I need professionals who demonstrate a long-term loyalty to their career. Concessions can be made if it is a *short-term* accommodation."

Corporations rarely, if ever, convey the truth about these accommodations. It is not necessarily true that taking advantage of alternative work schedules somehow jeopardizes an employee's job. Most executives believe that in today's working environment, a professional indeed can earn a living and do a competent job while working such a schedule. Still, when it comes to being identified as a top performer, or being offered promotional advancement, seizing opportunities to be away from the corporate environment will only hinder your career progression.

The Personal Cost of Success

While these executives could cite multiple examples of the impact their career demands had made on their spouses and children, it took some prodding in most cases to get them to articulate the effect these trade-offs had on them personally. My sense regarding their reluctance was not that they were being humble, but rather that they had never really stopped to ponder the question. Ultimately, most of the executives acknowledged that they really didn't have any hobbies or outside interests. In fact, many commented that they also did not have a large circle of friends. As one executive put it, "I'm at the age where I am thinking about retirement and wonder what I'll actually do or whom I'll do it with as I have so few friends." The demands of their careers have made it hard or even impossible for them to develop outside interests and an extensive social network—unless these were linked either to the job or industry.

The picture of executive life is not entirely bleak. Some interviewees played golf or tennis, and plenty who indeed did have friends. However, the overriding theme from this cadre is clear. Not only have they put themselves last behind their jobs, spouses, and children, many of them have never even factored their own interests into the equation. These individuals have devoted their entire professional lives to contributing substantially to an organization and tending to the needs of their families. In the process, they have lost a sense of themselves and their own needs. One executive shared this perspective: "If someone is driven to be a senior executive, they will define 'quality of life' differently from most people." While they enjoy professional recognition and financial success and even appreciate the creative and intellectual challenges their positions offer, there is, for the few that would admit it, a persistent sense of isolation.

Many of these successful folks described the loneliness that often accompanied their success. While these executives see themselves as the same people they have always been, their perception and treatment by others often changes over time. Those who climbed their way up through the corporate ranks said that this "arm's length" treatment by others in the organization often left them feeling isolated, longing for the days of laughing and joking with colleagues.

Other executives describe the realities of their role as, "Once an executive, always an executive." As one senior executive commented, "You reach a certain level and people expect you to act the same way all the time or assume you wear a suit twenty-four hours a day."

The point these executives are trying to make is that their persona always follows them. For example, one executive told me a story about being seen flying a kite with his children at a local park. A passerby recognized him and, calling him by name, shouted, "I can't believe you're actually here flying a kite!" This was as if to say that the executive should do nothing but work all day and night. Another interviewee relayed the story of the time he attended a company-sponsored fundraiser with his family. As it turned out, he was the only corporate officer in attendance and as a result was asked by the event coordinator to make a few opening remarks. He had to explain to the individual that he was uncomfortable with the request. He wasn't dressed appropriately, nor did he know much about the charitable organization. "I just told her that clearly there were far more knowledgeable people than myself to introduce the event."

These examples illustrate the burden and struggle of carrying these executive titles outside of the corporate walls. I recall a time when the father of a CEO I worked very closely with passed away. With repulsion, I watched the political maneuvering that went on amongst lower-level staff members to attend the funeral, as if the occasion was somehow the perfect opportunity to "see and be seen" by the executive cadre. As I sat quietly during the service, I remember thinking how difficult it must be for the CEO to reconcile his own personal grief with maintaining a stoic appearance in front of all these employees.

The lesson here is that being one of the world's most successful executives comes with the expectation that you maintain that persona in virtually every aspect of life. For those professionals with aspirations of holding such a position in the corporate world, be clear that this demand will often create challenges in maintaining your own authentic self. As one executive advises, "Figure out who you indeed want to be and how much of yourself you are willing to let go of to be successful."

No Time for Good Health

The other trade-off shared by some executives revolved around their health. In several cases, executives talked to the lack of time available for exercise or physical activity. In a few cases, executives suffered illnesses either during their career or later in life that they believe were a result of not focusing on their physical well being. One executive told me of a time when he had surgery to repair a double hernia. Contrary to the physician's advice, he demanded to be released from the hospital and drove himself to the office. As he remarked on his behavior, "I look back at that time and think 'How could I have been so reckless?' . . . but I was so driven about my work."

While a few of the executives interviewed commented that they consistently devote time to exercise, whether it be after work or during their workday, most commented that the demands of the job simply do not allow for such benefits. One female executive made this interesting comment: "If I could change anything about my journey to executive status, I would have taken better care of myself and my health. Male executives tend to better utilize their administrative assistants to coordinate their personal lives." She might be surprised at the number of male executives who contradicted that perspective. One such male executive said, "There are only so many hours in the day. Who has time to exercise?"

What was most interesting was that not a single executive alluded to the toll that job stress can take on personal health. From their perspective, the health setbacks these interviewees suffered correlated more to the lack of time available for physical activity than the intense pressure of the job itself. Considering the executives' remarks, it seems that these successful professionals are somehow impervious to the mental strain of their demanding positions. In fact, not only did the majority of these power players seem to withstand the pressure better than most "normal" professionals, they actually seemed to thrive on it!

The important message conveyed by many of these executives, particularly those over fifty years of age, is that executives must ensure that they are taking care of their health, no matter what the demands of the career. Otherwise, you run the risk of significant health issues later on in life, when you should be enjoying the fruits of all your years of hard work.

EXECUTIVE**SUMMARY**

The key lesson here for those professionals who are driven to attain senior-level jobs is to approach the journey with no blinders and to be fully cognizant of the sacrifices that will be demanded. Every corporate culture is different, but even if the messages sent from many corporations support achieving a balanced life, don't be misled. Success does not come in a forty-hour workweek. As our executives have already established, the higher you rise in an organization, the greater the demands on your time and the greater the need to make trade-offs.

Be sure that you have absolute clarity about your personal and professional goals, and decide if you are truly willing to make the necessary sacrifices to attain them. No one can make those decisions for you, and you should not be influenced by the opinions of others in the corporate world regarding your decisions. As one female executive eloquently put it, "Others don't define for me what balance is—I define it for myself and if they don't like it, too bad." Only the arrogant will attempt to tell you how and where your time should best be spent. The other critical message is that no matter the choice, you must own the decision and never look back. Operating with regret will only make for an unhappy family life *and* an unfulfilled work life. ◉

3 | INTELLIGENCE IS ONLY ONE VARIABLE IN THE EQUATION

Many working professionals share the belief that highly successful executives have exceptional intelligence. Having worked with a significant number of executives, I know that is not always true. In talking with the executives, at least half of those interviewed agreed with my opinion. As one person stated, "My initial assumption about senior management was that they were much smarter and more experienced than myself. This did not prove to be true. Although many of them had a higher level of education or a different level of external experience, I often found that they were no more effective and sometimes less effective than I expected." By their own standards, a larger number of the executives consider themselves to be of average or above-average intelligence. There were, in fact, a handful of executives who did consider themselves to be exceptionally bright. The qualifier to the executives' comments, however, is that the majority consider themselves highly knowledgeable in their specific area of expertise. In further probing the issue with the executives, I learned that regardless of their own perceived level of intelligence, most of them believe that they are equally intelligent and educated as most of the executive cadre. As one executive put it, "That's the thing about this level . . . you meet a lot of really smart people who humble you with their smarts and yet, they're humbled some days by what you know."

Analysis of the educational background of the executives interviewed showed that it ran the gamut. Seven percent of the executive group only had a high school education, while others held advanced degrees from prestigious schools such as MIT or Harvard. A number of these executives acknowledged that they were indeed top students, but there were also plenty of executives who stated they received average and sometimes below-average grades in college.

The point is not to say that education and grades are unimportant in reaching executive-level positions in today's corporate environment—they are extremely important. Instead, the point is to put the academic performance and credentials of these executives in context. Those executives who achieved a high level of success without a degree generally worked at a time when a high school diploma was competitive in the working world. Alternately, they worked in industries in which working your way up the corporate ladder was accomplished through on-the-job training.

The simple truth is that in today's competitive environment, a bachelor's degree is the equivalent of a high school diploma thirty years ago. Advanced degrees are almost a standard requirement for professional positions, so do not underestimate the importance of building a solid educational background. In and of itself, though, having a degree will guarantee you nothing beyond a competitive edge in entering the corporate workforce.

Focusing on Competence

As reinforced by the executives, there is a difference between what you know and how you are perceived in an organization. As one executive emphasized, "Intelligence is only one factor of success. I've seen plenty of colleagues who were extremely bright but were unable to translate their ideas into concrete actions." In some cases the exceptionally bright individuals were great at "waxing philosophic" about corporate strategies, but they never applied the conceptual to a tactical plan. Most executives further acknowledged that few, if any, executive-level jobs allow solely for the "think tank" approach without producing tangible results. The caveat for the highly intelligent is to understand that knowledge alone will not get you recognized in an organization until you can demonstrate an ability to translate that knowledge into real-world applications. As one executive flippantly remarked, "Intelligence is only a prerequisite in the corporate world . . . it's 'table stakes.' It is more about what you can do than what you know."

Other components that executives cite as being critical to overall competence include developing solid business knowledge; understanding the interdependence of one function with another; possessing a practical, common sense approach to the business; and, certainly, having effective communication and interpersonal skills.

It is important to note that depending on the discipline in which the executive worked, some competencies were more highly valued than others. For example, one executive commented that in the IT function, most professionals possess above-average intelligence and are technically superior, but at the same time tend to be socially challenged and introverted. The exceptional performers in the IT area demonstrate far more effective people skills when compared to their peers. IT roles require significant interaction with customers, both internally and externally. The IT professional who demonstrates the ability to work effectively with others, deal with ambiguity, understand different perspectives, and then deliver the desired system or application, separate themselves from their peers and ultimately achieve more senior-level positions.

It's Okay to Say "I Don't Get It"

The executives interviewed shared a very clear and objective self-assessment of their talents and shortcomings. Many stated that over the course of their careers, one of the biggest lessons learned was to openly acknowledge, without apology or embarrassment, when they did not understand an issue or piece of information. As one executive commented, "You quickly learn in the corporate world that no one knows everything!" Several of the executives further commented, however, that many corporate professionals—and particularly the younger ones—are often reluctant to show any sign of weakness. Thus, they simply pretend to comprehend certain concepts or ideas. As one executive commented, "I'm the first one to stand up and say, 'I don't get it' while others would prefer to just 'wing it.'" Another executive put it this way, "When you're young, you think that you know so much, but as you mature you realize that you really know so little."

Following along these same lines are the experiences many interviewees have had with peers and executives who simply try to act smarter than they actually are. As one senior executive remarked, "I am not afraid to say that I don't know something simply because I know that I can't know everything . . . . Candidly, though, some people at this level get caught up in wanting to appear to know everything." At a high level of success, the egos are often oversized even when it is unwarranted. The trick for the ambitious professional is to derive true success from authentic intelligence and knowledge rather than from disingenuous notions. The only way a professional will develop solid business knowledge is by openly seeking out information and admitting when a concept or idea is not understood. "Faking it" will only lead to embarrassment or, worse still, failure in the corporate world.

Learn the Business Inside and Out

The most significant advice given by these executives was the importance of broadening one's overall business knowledge, as it applies to an individual discipline as well as the functions that most significantly influence the success of a corporation. Regardless of their area of expertise, each executive seized opportunities and proactively sought to acquire knowledge in critical areas of the business—even if it was outside their immediate function. While it wasn't as if each executive developed a specific "plan" to go out and obtain the information, most of them stated that at various times in their careers they had to figure out how to obtain the desired knowledge.

It is easy to coach professionals to proactively learn the business, but it is far more important to define the specific steps necessary to broaden business knowledge. First and foremost, understand that the process will take work. As one executive counseled, "Resolve to do some tedious, time-consuming work. Digging into the business requires devoting attention to the details."

The first step, if you haven't already done so, is to obtain a copy of both the annual report and the 10-K report. While both documents contain key financial data, the 10-K report contains specific disclosures as required by the Securities and Exchange Commission (SEC). Then actually read them. Do not skim them or simply review the numbers. Read the material cover to cover. These reports are important resources because it is your company's own description of who it is—its objectives, its shareholders, its key people, its problems, and its results. Don't be alarmed if there are portions of the reports that you do not understand. In fact, you should highlight those elements that are unfamiliar to you, as well as identify specific questions that arise after reviewing the material.

Once you have a grasp of what you know and don't know, go seek out the experts who can explain it to you. Some readers may consider this advice a "no-brainer." I can tell you from personal experience, as well as from the experience of the executives interviewed, that while many professionals conceptually understand the merits of seeking out information from others in the corporation, very few professionals actually devote the time to conduct this type of research on their company. Many executives believe that the reasons why people don't seek out the expertise of others, particularly individuals they do not know, is that they think these people will somehow view them as stupid, or that the experts will not devote the time to helping them. Both assumptions are incorrect. As one executive retorted, "If someone in the corporation would think you are ignorant simply because you are seeking out information, they aren't someone you should be worried about in the first place."

As far as being concerned that the experts in a company won't take the time to answer your questions, this is a groundless fear as well. With very few exceptions, everyone loves to talk about what they do and what they know. This is particularly true if you frame the discussion so the individual is approached and perceived as an "expert." Additionally, the majority of the executives interviewed commented that they welcome any professional seeking knowledge and information about the business. As one senior executive remarked, "So few people seek out information beyond that which applies to their world, that I would never turn an employee away for wanting to learn more about the business."

The Experts You Need to Know

Don't always shoot for the top executive. The problem is not that the executives won't know the answers—depending upon the questions, however, they may be further removed from the specific details. As one executive put it, "Some people think that as executives we are the expert on everything and we're not. So I can choose to either give the employee a more general answer or direct them to a person who is more intimately involved with the particular issues." Also, ensure that your motives are pure in deciding on who to approach. Your decision should be motivated by the desire to find the most knowledgeable person or persons, rather than trying to obtain a forum with someone you believe could be influential in your career. This tactic is always transparent and executives, while being surprisingly accommodating about sharing expertise, despise having their time wasted.

As it relates to the fundamentals of the business and the financial results of the organization, your best bet is to start with the investor relations (IR) department, which is usually a part of the finance function. Meeting with a member of the IR group will assist you in better understanding the "hot buttons" of both the investor community and industry analysts.

Do Your Homework

If you seek out the time of these corporate experts, be prepared. No one has any time to waste, so be organized about the areas you wish to discuss. Provide the resource with an advanced outline of the questions and issues to review in advance. The person will be impressed by your preparation and know that you were thoughtful enough to maximize their time. Additionally, this kind of preparation creates an immediate positive impression about your approach to work as well as your genuine interest in learning about the business.

In addition to answering your questions, seek out additional resources. If, for example, you are discussing the debt-to-equity ratio or pretax profit percentage, understanding the calculations is only the first step. The greater learning opportunity is in understanding the corporate strategies and operational issues that directly impact the numbers. You need to identify those individuals who can talk about the bigger picture. As one executive simply put it, "Continue to seek out information until you begin to grasp a clear understanding of what is making the company money and what is costing the company money."

No Department Is an Island

As the executives expressed, an important part of competence is the ability to understand the connection of one function to another, as well as the goals of all functions to the overall success of the organization. One executive made the following analogy: "Think of the corporation as the orchestra and each department represents a different section of the orchestra. You can't make beautiful music unless all sections are performing at their peak."

The best way to develop this understanding, aside from working with each of the functions on a regular basis, is to schedule informational meetings with select professionals of each function. Again, you should prepare for these meetings with the same rigor that you demonstrated in getting ready for your meeting with IR or finance. Think about what you are interested in knowing about the department and the people who work there. What are their key strategies? How do they link these efforts to the overall strategies of the corporation? Is the function profit-generating, or is it a cost center? What are the issues or problems impacting employees' performance? To what extent are they impacted by the function in which you work? How would they describe the working relationship between your two functions? What functions are they most reliant on, and why?

The informational interview definitely helps you to begin to develop a broader working capital—that is, what you solidly understand about the business. It will also create some fortuitous by-products. First off, you will steadily begin to establish a reputation as being one who is genuinely interested and curious about the business. These meetings also serve as a natural springboard to develop potentially significant relationships with a variety of colleagues throughout the organization.

Never Underestimate the Power of the Written Word

In talking about the importance of good communication skills, many of the executives specifically addressed the importance of demonstrating effective writing skills. As one executive commented, "You don't get brownie points for quality writing, but when you can't write well, the reader—often your boss—will pay more attention to the lack of skill rather than the content presented."

Executives are appalled by the poor written communication skills of most professionals today. Several of the executives are also of the belief that many employees today possess a false sense of security about their writing skills. All too many believe they write well when, in fact, they do not. One executive told me a story about a time early on in his career, when he submitted what he considered to be a well-written position paper to his boss for review. As he stood in his boss's office, his boss briefly read a portion of the document then proceeded to crumble it up into a ball and throw it back at the executive. His boss then shouted, "This paper is horrible and is a waste of my time. You can do better, so go back and fix it."

For all the time that professionals devote to getting an education and developing a breadth of business knowledge, most executives lament that these same folks underestimate the power of the written word. As one executive remarked, "Too many young professionals believe they have good written communication skills when they actually don't!" In the business world, strong writing skills are critical to the ability to effectively communicate ideas and opinions. In today's business climate, where e-mails are often the primary means of communication, writing skills are often one of the first ways to establish credibility as a communicator. In the absence of this skill, even the brightest and most knowledgeable individual may never achieve the recognition or career growth necessary to achieving corporate success.

EXECUTIVE SUMMARY

By their own admission, many of the executives reinforced that an individual can indeed be successful in the corporate world without meeting membership requirements for Mensa. In fact, many of the executives interviewed have observed professionals of average intelligence achieve great success, while many exceptionally bright individuals often fail in the business world. Perhaps the most important factor for increasing a competitive edge in the corporate arena is developing a broader understanding of the financial drivers of a corporation. By developing a greater understanding of key financial indicators, the implications of short- and long-term strategies on fiscal performance, and the specific objectives of each function in a corporation, you can take a more deliberate approach to seeking out opportunities to provide greater contribution and value to an organization. Simply put, it is from the acquisition of this knowledge that you begin to build a platform for long-term career success. ⊙

4 | READING THE CORPORATE LANDSCAPE

A significant number of the executives I interviewed reinforced the importance for professionals of understanding the specific culture or "landscape" of their company. Unfortunately, such insights are not provided in the employee handbook or reviewed during a new-hire orientation. As a result, most employees do not understand how to get the lay of the land, as it relates to achieving success in the corporate world.

We have discussed the importance of understanding the drivers of a corporation as it relates to building a successful career, but equally important is the ability to understand the organizational dynamics, corporate politics, and "power players" that exist in an organization. These elements are critical to your career success in that they can influence your visibility within the corporation and are a major factor in garnering recognition and rewards.

Every corporate culture has its own personality. Some are highly subversive, or passive aggressive, while others are more open to healthy exchanges between professionals. It's important that you pay attention to the cultural behavior of your company and ask yourself the following critical questions about the environment:

Does the culture value ideas? To what extent does management promote and reward the healthy exchange of ideas or approaches to the business?

Is the organization nurturing? That is, does it allow for mistakes and focus on the development of its professionals?

Is the environment hierarchical? Are you free to discuss ideas and interact at all levels, or must you operate within a rigid chain of command?

Does the culture promote cross-functional development? Does the environment allow for lateral moves to other disciplines? Are there living examples of professionals who have successfully transferred across functions in the organization?

Do you feel safe to make comments or share contrary opinions? Does management respect contradictory recommendations or ideas? Does the culture value spirited debate on issues?

While typically it is corporation leaders who conduct a cultural survey as a means of determining whether the company is operating under its desired value and belief system, individual professionals would be well served to conduct their own informal surveys. One of the best ways to evaluate the specific behaviors and values of a corporation is to find and take a cultural survey. As your company's HR department may have administered one of these in the past, they may be able to help you get one. If you are uncomfortable in asking for the survey, a number of companies sell such tools via the Internet.

The value of a cultural survey is in its ability to give you focus. The process of finding and taking one of these surveys on your own will give you an organized, comprehensive list of questions about corporate culture. Answering these will help you ask the right questions about your organization, which in turn will help you identify those corporate values and behaviors that are most important to you and a flourishing career.

Given that your chosen career will require a major devotion in terms of time, it is imperative to select a corporate culture you enjoy working in and that allows you to thrive. Be uncompromisingly honest with yourself when it comes to deciding what type of an environment that is. Some professionals enjoy the machinations of corporate politics. They find the game of positioning themselves within an organization or industry as exciting as the work itself, while others find it contrived and distasteful. As one executive put it, "You have to decide if you want to expend the energy necessary to be effective in your organization." If you find your current corporate culture too difficult to manage, then it is time to find another company with a different culture. As many of the executives commented, professionals forget that they have choices. Too often, they allow themselves to feel trapped in a contradictory culture. One executive said, "When you are talented, there are far more options and corporations available to you in your career. You can indeed pick and choose . . . it is in finding the most conducive corporate culture that your career will thrive."

Corporate Politics: Good Versus Evil

Too often, professionals in the corporate world attribute negative connotations to the word "politics." How often have you heard someone say, "Oh, he's so political," or "I don't play politics!" Most working professionals know political behavior when they see it. But when asked to describe corporate politics, most have to stop and think about the true definition of the concept.

In discussing the issue with executives during the interview process, most had a firm grasp of corporate politics and expressed a clear definition of the concept. As one executive eloquently defined it, "Politics is when the *who* becomes more important than the *what*"—that is to say, when the individual's motivation is personal rather than focused on the overall objective of the corporation. Understand, however, that there is a difference between the strategy of managing politics and that of operating as a political animal. It simply comes down to motivation. Managing corporate politics is a defensive yet proactive approach to maneuvering through a corporate environment. "Being" political, on the other hand, is a deliberate and conscious choice to drive self-interest over business success. Most of the executives interviewed consider themselves politically savvy, but they don't waste their time on personal agendas. As one executive shared, "We are vehicles for the corporation to perform. It is about the success of the company, not my personal agenda. If you've got the right motives and objectives, it isn't about a 'me versus you' issue."

While many professionals are quick to criticize the corporate world for being overly political, this perspective is rather naïve. As several executives reinforced, politics are an inevitable part of the corporate landscape. It is a work-related behavior that is important to understand. Otherwise, you run the risk of being blindsided by the personal objectives of colleagues who have the potential to hinder your effectiveness in the workplace. Let's be clear—the executives interviewed here do not advocate any professional act with political motivation. They do, however, acknowledge that political behavior is an everyday part of working in the corporate world. As one executive commented, "Put any three people together, and there will be political dynamics . . . it's human nature."

If anyone were to ask me if I had ever acted politically in the course of my career, the answer would be, "Of course I did." One cannot survive, let alone flourish, in the corporate world without developing a level of political savvy. This understanding requires the ability to identify the personal motivations of others and to modify your approach accordingly. For example, one of the best lessons any mentor ever taught me was to determine the outcome of a meeting before I even entered the room. In too many instances, I would simply approach a meeting assuming that my knowledge would influence the desired outcome, only to be blindsided by personal agendas or arguments. Through the guidance of a mentor, I learned to spend time with all of the interested parties, and certainly those key players who could influence decisions, to understand all of their issues and concerns. This insight allowed me to better prepare for the meeting and positioned me to address specific issues. This informed approach ultimately helped create a more congenial discussion and often resulted in a more effective outcome.

After you accept the inevitability of politics in the corporate dynamic, the question then becomes, "How do I identify the personal motivations of others?" The easiest way to recognize personal agendas is to interact with your colleagues on a regular basis. The more time you devote to discussing company objectives and their implications on various functions, the more quickly specific agendas and potential barriers begin to surface.

In addition, the more time you spend with an individual, the more likely you are to identify patterns of behavior. What are a particular colleague's motivations? Is he interested in getting resources for his department, or positioning himself for another promotion? Does she want to set the agenda, or to keep quiet and not stick her neck out until she sees which way the group is going? Active listening skills are a critical element to achieving this objective. As one executive remarked,

"It's no coincidence that human beings were given two ears and only one mouth."

Beyond listening to and observing your colleagues, being politically savvy requires that you consciously build alliances with peers around specific strategies. Even at those times when peers "agree to disagree," a clear understanding of the areas of disagreement arms you with critical points for discussion and influence. This knowledge allows you to wield influence from a far better bargaining position, as compared to having the issues unexpectedly surface in a meeting.

Some working professionals are critical of this "political" approach and believe that such tactics are a waste of time. However, many of the executives interviewed disagree. They counter by saying that in not taking this approach, working professionals run the risk of wasting far more time as a result of having to reposition and repackage their opinions and arguments.

Examining Your Motives

When I worked in HR, professionals often approached me in search of advice and guidance on how to effectively interact and influence others, including their bosses. In one case, a vice president sought my counsel on effectively communicating her business strategies to her boss, an executive vice president (EVP). Their previous meetings had been less than effective, and the EVP was beginning to take issue with her ability to manage the business. As I too worked closely with the EVP,

I provided the subordinate with some approaches that I had found to be very effective in my own dealings with him. The vice president employed the strategies, and the subsequent meeting with her boss proved to be a very positive one.

Shortly thereafter, a few colleagues gave me the "heads up" that the EVP had been asking questions about my conduct in meetings and for specifics about what I had said about him. Not surprisingly, I was later summoned to his office to discuss my coaching of his employee. Essentially, the EVP was taking issue with the influencing strategies I had provided to his employee, which she apparently had shared with him. Although he didn't say it outright, essentially he was accusing me of being political. He believed that my coaching was promoting political behavior on the part of his subordinate. I, on the other hand, was surprised by his assessment and considered his perspective to be both immature and naïve. I explained to him that in my role, it was common to have a variety of employees seek objective guidance on dealing with all levels of colleagues in the organization, including their supervisors. I apologized, since the discussion had led him to question my personal motives, but reassured him that such coaching was a critical part of my contribution to the organization. Interestingly enough, we ended up cultivating a very strong working relationship; in fact, he often sought similar insights relating to his own direct reports.

This example illustrates an important point. Even those professionals who are motivated to "do the right thing" sometimes inadvertently create situations that some will perceive as political. While the perception other people have of you is often beyond your control, you must constantly question your own personal motives to ensure that your interests are in support of the corporation, rather than a self-serving agenda.

EXECUTIVE**SUMMARY**

A key lesson for any professional is to acknowledge that political behavior exists everywhere, and the corporate world is no exception. The good news is that each and every corporate culture influences the degree to which politics exists in the organization. As a result, you must strive to find a corporation whose culture is most congruent with your own belief system.

The other critical insight to remember is that while you cannot control the actions of others, you can control your own motivation and conduct in the working world. Interestingly enough, the executives interviewed all demonstrated a genuine sense of self. They could often relate situations in which they had to decide whether to stay true to themselves or to acquiesce to the politics of the situation. The majority of the executives expressed that they ultimately found that competence and candor usually prevailed over selfish interest and personal agenda. As one executive put it, "It's the people who lack self-confidence who resort to political tactics . . . when you can stand on your own two feet, there is no need to be political." ⊙

5 | GENERALIST VERSUS SPECIALIST: TAKING THE BROADER VIEW

Most professionals immediately equate success in the corporate world with promotions in title, position, and financial compensation. While upward advancement is undeniably important, astute professionals consider such advancement within the larger context of their overall career strategies. As many of the executives interviewed noted, advancement should not be an end in and of itself—gaining knowledge about the company, industry, and key players should be. That, in the long-term, will serve the needs of the corporation as well as personal ambition.

When seeking advancement, you must make a conscious decision about whether to pursue a specialist or generalist career track. Most professionals understand the definition of a business specialist—one who is focused upon a specific body of knowledge or area of business expertise. The true definition of a business generalist, however, is often far more difficult for individuals to understand, let alone to develop in the workplace.

The executives interviewed all have an area that they consider to be a specialty. Yet virtually all of these successful individuals talked in great detail about how, in addition to their core competence, they have acquired a broader business background. They also emphasized the significance of this strategy in their achievement of senior level positions. As the executives explained, the ability to cultivate a well-rounded perspective of the business, and its specific drivers, increases one's contribution to an organization and leads to more strategic-level roles. As one executive commented, "The ability to create value to a corporation is to incorporate the perspectives of other disciplines into one's decision-making process."

The executives went on to say that, in most cases, those who do take the path of a business generalist do not do so by conscious choice. Rather, the choice just grew out of a genuine interest, passion, and curiosity for the business as a whole. Their primary motivation was to create opportunities to influence significant change in their respective companies, rather than seizing the broader experiences as a means of getting to the top. This is an important lesson for professionals to understand, as building a generalist background requires taking a certain level of risk. This risk stems from stepping out of one's own area of comfort into realms that are both unknown and not necessarily guaranteed to result in success or immediate recognition and respect.

While both the generalist and the specialist strategies offer the potential for promotion and significant rewards, the majority of executives interviewed believe that the generalist background holds the greatest career potential in an organization. In my own experience, I have also found that the generalist is more likely to receive promotions more often than the specialist. For example, there was a time in my career when I, along with one of my peers, was being considered for promotion to vice president. When I learned there was only one vice president promotion to be approved in the department, I told the senior vice president that the promotion should be given to my colleague. His business results had had far greater fiscal impact for the company, and he had far more tenure in the position. My boss concurred with my opinion. Much to my surprise, however, I received the promotion after all. I later learned that one of the driving factors for the senior executives who approved the promotion was that I provided the corporation with expertise in all aspects of human resources. My peer, on the other hand, while exceptional in his role, was a true specialist in the areas of employee benefits and insurance.

Seeing the Bigger Picture

Even when a business specialist is content with being a specialist, there are still benefits to understanding the broader picture of the business. Indeed, all of the executives interviewed capitalized on various opportunities to participate outside their area of expertise. This was an excellent means of increasing influence and impacting the business in a more direct way.

The goal of broadening one's own business scope is perhaps most important to those professionals who operate as specialists in a staff function versus a line function. Line functions are those that directly impact the bottom-line performance of the organization, such as the sales department of a company; staff functions, on the other hand, are those that support the organization but do not directly influence the financial performance or generate revenue for the corporation. Finance, human resources, marketing, and information technology are just a few examples of traditional staff functions. If you have chosen a career in a staff function, it does not mean that your career success is limited. Many senior-level executives have flourished in staff functions—just ask any chief information officer. However, unless a specialist can demonstrate a comprehensive understanding of the business, and successfully link his or her efforts to key business initiatives, the potential for advancement will be stifled.

Hedging Your Bets

While there is nothing wrong with being a business specialist, it is important to understand that this career strategy does have limitations and potential risks. One IT executive shared an example involving mainframe programmers.

Before personal computers became prevalent, mainframe programmers used to be the "special ones" in the IT world. Over time, the mainframe programmers became regarded as obsolete and were viewed as dinosaurs. The executive explained that when he coached the programmers to learn the new technology, they were often very reluctant to make the change. The programmers argued that essentially they were being asked to "start over" in their careers. What many of these professionals did not realize, however, was that their careers were already being hindered as a result of their chosen specialty.

Another executive described the risks associated with a specialist track this way: "If you pick a specialty, you're betting that it's going to be the winning horse. The likelihood of that happening in a corporation is slim. Therefore, you want to be able to demonstrate more things . . . so when things change [in a company or industry], you have the flexibility to continue to add value." Breadth, not always depth, of knowledge, is the key to career security and advancement.

Lateral Moves on the Way to the Top

In discussing the approaches that they implemented in developing a generalist background, more than half of interviewees talked about the significance that lateral moves played in achieving that objective. They emphasized, however, that for lateral moves to be positive for one's career, you must truly understand the position's long-term impact on your career. That is, you must clearly see the merit of the move to your overall goals and development. As one executive conveyed, "If you just make the move without a true desire for the job, and little understanding of how it fits into the overall scheme, the risk is that you won't perform well or you will end up hating the job. Either way, you're going to end up leaving the organization because of an uninformed choice."

Several of the executives also admitted the reality that oftentimes an organization is simply more concerned about placing the most effective person in the job rather than considering the implications for that individual's career objectives. One executive put it the following way: "I wish somebody would have told me when I was floundering around thinking that the company had my best interest at heart, that oftentimes they really don't. The truth is that often management doesn't have a grand scheme for your career. They are busy people. You have to have your best interest in mind. After all, it's your career."

That being said, several executives expressed the opinion that professionals should not underestimate the value of taking a lateral move for the organization, even in a situation where the professional does not see the long-term value of the career move to his or her overall success. The fact is that sometimes an organization has a critical problem. As one executive remarked, "They have a hole in the organization and they want you to fill that need . . . It's that simple." While under these circumstances the move may indeed be risky, the recognition you achieve by rescuing the corporation might clearly outweigh any potential risks in the long run. In addition, it gives you valuable credit to bargain for assignments that you *do* want. Just don't spend an indefinite period of time in such assignments or take several of them in succession, as that could end up deferring your own career objectives permanently. The best strategy is to tie the assignment to measurable company objectives—such as getting an office up and running, or restoring a business unit to profitability.

While the executives encouraged professionals to ask questions about the merits of the lateral move, they also suggested not being overly concerned about the length of the assignment. Professionals need to be careful not to become overly focused about the time commitment of the new position, as that behavior sends the wrong message to senior management—not the least of which is that you may shirk the duties of the position due to impatience or boredom. The only exception to this advice was an assignment requiring physical relocation, as such moves have an impact not only on the professional but on family as well. In such cases, it is completely acceptable to obtain the general time frame for the assignment.

Success Is Not Always a Straight Line

The other lesson the executives offered with regard to lateral moves is that professionals should not shy away from transferring into areas where they have no experience. Several executives remarked that often professionals are prone to remain in jobs that are comfortable without "stretching" to learn a new area. The executives further reinforced the importance of not being fearful to try something new. One executive drew this analogy: "Why does the kid ride his bike across the top of a fence? Because he thinks he can and has no fear about doing it."

In their own experience, most of the executives interviewed found that taking job opportunities in new areas proved to be far more advantageous to their careers than playing it safe. One executive, for example, shared a personal experience about working with a company that asked him to move from marketing to corporate planning. "While I had never considered the corporate planning function, I trusted the people who thought I would be successful in the job. They had identified me for the position and so I took the chance. The job ended up being one of most pivotal roles in my career. I loved it." This example illustrates an all-too-important issue—trust. As several of the executives commented, taking the "leap" into areas of uncertainty requires that you trust in those individuals driving corporate career moves. These successful professionals are not suggesting that you blindly and naively assume that all in the working world can be trusted to manage with your best interest in mind, but they do reinforce that sometimes taking a chance on a proposed career move is definitely worth the risk.

It is also critical to understand that being overly selective about your career moves can have repercussions. While every executive has the right to decline a position, often this privilege is a one-shot deal. In many corporate cultures, once you decline a positional move along the corporate ladder, it is rarely offered again.

Some executives even shared examples of taking a step backward as a means of getting ahead in a corporation. One executive shared her decision to move from a prestigious corporate marketing position to a brand management role. The opportunity gave her broader experiences, beyond traditional marketing into areas of sales promotions and development of collateral material. The career move proved instrumental in her obtaining an executive-level marketing position.

The reality check is that sometimes you have to be willing to make sacrifices in the short-term for the potential of greater long-term rewards. Several executives shared examples of making lateral moves that offered no additional compensation and that sometimes even required a reduction in pay. I recall one executive who accepted a 20 percent pay cut because he believed that the position was critical to his overall success. Many of these same executives however, reaped far greater financial rewards from the short-term sacrifices, as those jobs often served as a springboard to immediate promotion. If your goal is to achieve greater responsibility, no matter what your discipline, the challenge then becomes how to build a broader base of experiences that will be valued by your corporation and ultimately lead to a senior-level position.

As the executives spoke about the importance of experiencing a variety of assignments and job opportunities over the course of one's career, they conveyed an underlying message. Building a successful career requires clarity about one's professional goals and the personal conviction to stay true to those objectives. For example, one executive shared an experience about when she was asked to transfer into a field-level sales position. As she explained, "I was candid about the fact that I wouldn't be happy in certain markets. I realized that I might have shot myself in the foot, but I stayed true to what I wanted."

What Goes Up Often Must Come Down

When it comes to lateral moves, one of the most common "pushbacks" executives experience is that employees are more preoccupied with immediate advancement than developing a broad base of experience. However, engineering promotions too quickly can lead to disaster. As one executive commented, "Some people just want the title, position, and money and then assume that the knowledge, wisdom, and experience will somehow jump into their heads. It just doesn't work that way."

In my own career as a senior-level executive, I observed a colleague who campaigned for a director-level job until she finally received the promotion. Within a year, she failed in the position because she did not possess the skills required in the job. This failure resulted in two significant outcomes. She lost her job, and then she found it incredibly difficult to secure a comparable position in the marketplace. The simple truth was that her "tool kit" was missing far more wrenches than other candidates applying for the same job.

This example illustrates the need for professionals to carefully manage career choices and not to be too quick to grab for the brass ring. Today's promotion can often lead to tomorrow's termination.

EXECUTIVE SUMMARY

The key to building a successful career is patience. A professional must understand that achieving senior-level positions in a corporation takes time. When you consider that over 60 percent of the executives interviewed are over the age of fifty, it becomes apparent that there are no shortcuts to achieving success.

Success is never instantaneous. It requires a thoughtful and mature approach to building a comprehensive level of skill and experience. While admirable, the desire to achieve an influential position and acquire all the rewards that accompany such positions must also be supported by a genuine commitment to develop and contribute to an organization.

In most cases, impatient professionals are driven by personal motivations at the expense of seeking out valuable work experiences. As most of the executives commented, while this self-serving strategy may provide some short-term rewards for the individual, in the long run, it will only prove to hinder career growth and achievement of true corporate success. ◉

6 | PLAYING THE VICTIM GETS YOU NOWHERE

In any discussion of corporate success, the talk tends to revolve around developing competencies and delivering tangible results in the workplace. However, success also requires that professionals demonstrate a proactive approach in maneuvering through an organization and developing their careers. Many of the executives interviewed expressed frustration around highly competent professionals who constantly played the victim in virtually every aspect of their career. No matter what happened to these victims, good or bad, it was either never enough or it was always someone else's fault.

In extensive discussions with the executives about this mentality, they described the following three most common victim-related behaviors:

- Entitlement
- The blame game
- Looking out for Numero Uno

In describing the profile of a typical employee who might succumb to demonstrating these counterproductive behaviors, most of the executives reinforced that the role of corporate victim crosses all demographic boundaries—young and old, male and female, long-tenured and newly hired—disruptive employees come in all forms.

The Entitlement Mentality

When the executives described the entitlement mentality, they referred to the victim's expectation that the corporation will manage and direct his or her career. While they conveyed that this behavior tends to be more common amongst younger professionals, the executives have also observed this behavior in employees with long tenures. As managers of people, these successful leaders indeed believe it to be the charter of a corporation to develop and cultivate talent. They further commented, however, that the true responsibility for achieving a successful career must rest squarely on the shoulders of the professional. As one executive put it, "No one except yourself has a vested interest in your success." Another executive shared this opinion: "You have to believe in your own destiny and take responsibility to make it happen."

Several of the executives noted that more often than not, the professionals demonstrating an entitlement mentality were not even cognizant of their behavior—or the lack of respect it engendered with peers, colleagues, and their management team. The harsh reality for the entitlement victim is that all too often this behavior stalls any career opportunities before it is possible for the victim to demonstrate any inherent value to the organization.

The other interesting observation made by many of the executives is that those individuals who expect others to drive their success typically tend to be less than stellar performers. As one executive commented, "It's always the mediocre people who have such a sense of entitlement. You look at the people who make the noise, create the lawsuits—they're average at best. Though they may not realize it, their career is headed into the ditch."

As it relates to the younger professional, many of the executives attribute their sense of entitlement to the advantages afforded to them in their everyday lives. They remarked that many of the younger employees had been raised in households that provided far more luxuries, financial affluence, and stability than the executives had experienced at a similar age. As one executive illustrated, "Most of the younger employees grew up in a home that provided a bathroom for every bedroom. I grew up with several siblings and our house had only one bathroom." Another executive commented, "I see entry-level employees driving expensive cars they received from their parents for graduation. I didn't have a car until I was in my twenties and I had to buy it myself."

In citing these examples, these executives were clearly not attempting to begrudge the younger employees their advantages. Rather, they were attempting to illustrate how the "getting what you want, when you want it" mindset is cultivated in the younger generation. As described in the opening chapters, many of these executives profiled are in their mid-fifties. They grew up in low- to middle-income families and lived in fairly modest homes. If they wanted something new, they clearly understood that they, not others, would be responsible for providing it. They were never afforded a free ride or any other sense of entitlement.

Executives also distinguished the corporate cultures in which they began and grew their careers from those now available to younger professionals. The majority of these executives worked in corporations where little or no succession-planning or career-development efforts were provided to professionals. In today's corporate climate, the good news is that many corporations do indeed devote time and resources to developing the talent of their employees and preparing people for their next positions. As one executive remarked, "We [corporations] have a vested interest in developing talent . . . it's too competitive [in industry] to lose the good ones."

That said, however, even in organizations that successfully manage the succession-planning process, this mechanism in and of itself does not guarantee that every professional will benefit from the program. Younger professionals must still contend with establishing themselves as high-potential employees.

What was most enlightening was that at least half of the executives interviewed asserted that the corporations themselves often perpetuate this entitlement mentality. As one executive commented, "Sometimes we [companies] do too much handholding." In creating programs that support the needs of their employees, corporations can inadvertently create the misconception that they will take care of the employee's career. Examples of such programs include structured mentoring programs and alternative work schedules.

While many of the executives interviewed believe that corporations should genuinely attempt to provide guidance and developmental support to professionals, they also stressed that it was important for individuals not to rely on this support as the sole means of getting ahead in the corporate world. Companies are too busy and have far too many employees to oversee. The tremendous demands required by today's managers make it very difficult, if not impossible, for anyone to remain focused on the careers of every individual in their employ. Moreover, in today's often-cutthroat corporate environment, managers must often be more concerned with their own professional survival than the career development of their employees—particularly if they feel that a subordinate's promotion may diminish their own position. The simple fact is that to achieve success, you must take responsibility for your own career. Corporate resources should be considered as a supplemental tool rather than the primary source of your success in the corporate world.

The Blame Game

The evil twin of entitlement is a behavior several of the executives labeled as the "blame game." Like the entitlement mentality, the professional views the corporation, and its leaders, as being responsible for managing his or her career. Beyond that, however, these individuals fault everyone but themselves for adverse career outcomes. Examples of this behavior provided by the executives include such familiar statements as "I was passed over because they didn't like me" and "The company never gave me a chance." This attitude not only perpetuates an unsuccessful career for the victim, in many cases it results in absolute failure in the job due to a lack of interest by higher-ups to champion your cause or contribute to your success. As one executive put it, "The 'blamer' is very often left out in the cold."

Beyond the importance of taking personal responsibility for your overall career choices, the need for personal accountability also applies to individual performance. The executives confided that too often they observe staff members blaming their mistakes and career obstacles on others without taking ownership for their contribution to a problem or bad decision. As one executive relayed, "I've worked with plenty of people who resorted to 'ass-kissing' or finger-pointing because they just weren't smart enough to stand on their own two feet."

The reality is that far too many professionals harbor the erroneous fear that the admission of mistakes somehow hinders their career. Each executive could recall a time when they were the cause of a problem and had to stand up and take responsibility for the mistake. In virtually every instance, taking personal responsibility resulted in gaining greater respect from their superiors. As managers of people, many executives also learned that demonstrating personal accountability reinforced and cultivated the same behavior from their staff.

Executives further commented that the blame game is particularly detrimental to the development of strong working relationships with peers. Once a peer observes a colleague conducting himself in a fashion of self-preservation and dishonesty, they will begin to avoid or "work around" the individual. The executives further stated that even when peers were required to work with the blamer, most of them were reluctant to share information or provide any assistance to the person. As one executive commented, "Believe me, you need your peers to be on your side." Political capital is one of the most important currencies for getting things accomplished in an organization—you don't want to expend it pointing fingers at others.

The point here is that everyone, even the most senior executives, makes mistakes during their career. Taking personal responsibility for your actions, rather than finger-pointing, earns far more respect from influential individuals as a means of defending your performance. When a professional can display personal maturity and integrity, business leaders are more apt to promote that individual into leadership roles that can set positive examples and influence the behavior of many employees.

In deeper discussions with the executives the issue of finger-pointing, a number of the executives spoke about being on the receiving end of the finger point. Those executives advise professionals to take the experience in stride—the facts usually surface one way or another. That said, however, several of the executives strongly believe in setting the record straight when falsely accused of being the source of a problem or mistake. As one remarked, "Sometimes it is worth it to defend yourself and let the world know who is accountable and who is making excuses."

Looking Out for Numero Uno

One commonality amongst the executives interviewed was a genuine desire to serve their corporations and shareholders in an honest and significant way. In describing their personal style, many said they were never hesitant to share a contrary opinion when they truly believed that doing so enabled them to act as good stewards to the organization. They also said that such candor occasionally made it difficult for them personally and did engender hostility and resistance from colleagues on certain occasions. However, all of them stated that they felt it was more important to stand firm in their convictions—despite criticism. They believed that enduring criticism was sometimes a necessary trade-off when it came to honoring their convictions—and their commitment to the organization.

Those individuals, on the other hand, who consistently look out for number one often conduct themselves in a manner that is self-serving and designed to protect their professional power base. Despite the strong personal ambition of the executives interviewed, almost all of them expressed a strong sense of disdain, and even disgust, for such individuals as such behavior did not demonstrate a genuine desire to serve the organization. Moreover, it is something that quickly becomes all too apparent to peers and superiors.

The important lesson for the professional to remember is not to confuse driving one's career with the behavior of looking out for number one. It is vital that you make conscious choices about your career path. Such behavior refers to the way in which you conduct yourself in the job: your actions, decisions, opinions, and results. When self-interest becomes the primary driver, you can bet that your actions are not supporting the overall objectives of the organization—a fact that will be recognized by those above you.

EXECUTIVE SUMMARY

If you are ever recognized as being driven by personal agendas rather than the best interest of the corporation, it becomes very difficult to overcome that stigma in an organization. In effect, your career will be over before it even starts. Take an honest and critical look at your behavior and expectations. Are you expecting a third party, whether a manager or an organization, to manage your career and provide opportunities? Get feedback from a trusted peer to see if you are exhibiting such behavior. If so, make a concerted effort to correct your interactions. If you feel uncomfortable seeking out such constructive criticism, don't worry, there will always be plenty of bosses willing to provide you with that honest and critical feedback. If you're lucky, you will hear it at a performance review, but more than likely, it will take the form of a lack of respect and diminished professional advancement within the organization. ◉

I n my many years of coaching employees on performance issues, I have been amazed by their naiveté in believing that hard work in and of itself will lead to increased visibility in an organization. As several of the executives reinforced, establishing one's credibility as a hard-working and reliable performer does serve as a platform for increased visibility in an organization. However, they also stressed a corollary point. While your ability to demonstrate significant effort is indeed important to overall performance, the unvarnished truth is that hard work, in and of itself, does not guarantee recognition by those who influence career success. What drives career success is visibility—and the support of key executives in your organization. They must want success for you as much as you want it for yourself.

While many of the executives interviewed believe that gaining exposure to key executives does indeed play a role in achieving success in the corporate world, they also counsel professionals to be cautious in their approach to acquiring such recognition. When professionals are motivated more by gaining personal visibility than a genuine concern for the business, they run the risk of being perceived as "grandstanders." Senior executives are inherently skeptical of those employees who seek out every opportunity to meet with them one-on-one. As one executive commented, "You see the people who want to meet with you for the wrong reasons. I get employees who call and get on my calendar under the guise of a work matter, but then it becomes apparent that they are there under false pretense. What that person really wants is to be seen. Personally, I stay away from employees who take that approach."

When we talk about creating opportunities to naturally, over the course of doing business, connect with influential individuals in a corporation, the question then becomes other than performing well in one's job, how do you accomplish this goal?

Step out of the Box!

A number of the executives interviewed shared the opinion that there is an effective means of gaining visibility. The professional must seize every opportunity to become involved in business issues and assignments that extend beyond his or her normal scope of responsibility. As one executive stated, "Don't labor in obscurity—being reserved will not serve you well in your career."

Special Projects

The good news is that numerous projects exist in corporations that allow an individual to differentiate themselves from the rest of the working population. For example, you can volunteer to lead a special project for the company. As one executive shared, "Spearheading an important project allows you to put yourself in front of the right people and a cross-section of the corporation." Exposure to executives and decision-makers in other parts of the organization can provide you with additional opportunities for learning, expand your network within the organization, and possibly provide opportunities for lateral moves and advancement.

Cross-Functional Assignments

A professional's participation in business initiatives that cut across a broad range of different departments can create many opportunities to gain recognition by both peers and superiors across the organization. As we have already learned, most executives believe in the merits of developing knowledge about all areas of the company. Your involvement in interdepartmental assignments provides the perfect opportunity to develop a broader sense of the business. From a relationship standpoint, the added benefit of such programs is the opportunity to build critical alliances across the organization. As the executives reinforced, these cultivated relationships prove vital to one's success in the workplace.

Executive- or Company-Sponsored Programs

The majority of executives further shared that in the course of their own careers, they actively participated in select programs that the corporate culture conveyed were important. As one executive explained, "If we had a fundraiser, I was there. If my company was involved in Junior Achievement, I got involved." It is also important to note that often these programs are the pet projects of key executives in the company. Oftentimes, executives are as competitive in their philanthropic efforts as they are in business. One executive relayed a story in which he learned that his executive vice president was very committed to the United Way campaign. Essentially, the boss had mandated that his subordinates (of which the executive was one) contribute a specific amount to the charitable effort. Many of his colleagues complained that they thought it was wrong to contribute to a charitable organization just because it was "politically correct." This executive felt it was a worthwhile cause that also happened to be important to a senior executive. He contributed to the campaign and was recognized by the executive for his contribution to the cause. Interestingly enough, those employees who did not contribute found themselves being summoned into the EVP's office and told (in no uncertain terms) that either they contribute to the campaign or there would be repercussions.

Such an example illustrates the importance of demonstrating your personal involvement in and support of all those "special" causes in the corporate world. As one executive put it, "If you identify a project or initiative that is important to a key player in the company, and you don't have a moral or ethical dilemma about the program, you might want to consider getting actively involved in the project." Not only will your participation create opportunities to interact with these influential people, you often get to know these executives outside the corporate arena and cultivate personal relationships with them. As one executive put it, "These projects give you a chance to see executives as real people, without their corporate façade."

To the Rescue!

A number of the executives suggested that another way of gaining visibility was by seizing opportunities to assist senior executives with their problems and weaknesses. As one executive conveyed, "Tremendous opportunity for visibility exists when you can provide assistance to a senior executive who is operating outside of their comfort zone." One example provided by an executive involved his CEO, who was very ineffective when speaking to market analysts and the investor community. Part of the executive's role included the opportunity to coach the CEO. As a result, he gained the CEO's respect and developed a substantial working relationship with the top executive.

In my own personal experience, I worked with an executive vice president who would convene quarterly meetings with his division. While a very bright man, it became apparent during these meetings that he was less skilled and appeared visibly nervous when speaking to a group. Prior to one meeting, one of his direct reports gave him a laser pointer to assist in highlighting the profit and loss figures during his presentation. As the executive stood at the podium reviewing the financial results, everyone could see the red laser line wavering from his shaking hand. I could feel myself becoming flushed in embarrassment for him and was mortified as I watch his staff exchange glances from across the room. At the end of the meeting, I made it my personal mission to help this man, who I dearly respected, with this shortcoming.

My challenge however, was to provide that assistance without embarrassing him and committing career suicide in the process. One has to remember that most successful people, and certainly executives, do have (often huge) egos. Fortunately, he later asked me how I thought the meeting had gone. I told him that I thought the material was very comprehensive but that the laser pointer, being a new gadget, was detracting from the information being presented. I went on to suggest that with all of the meetings he would be conducting, perhaps it would be wise to hire a consultant to assist him.

To depersonalize the issue, I deliberately focused on providing a resource to assist on the substance of the presentations rather than his delivery. He was very receptive to the idea and within a few weeks he had hired the person I had recommended. Beyond that point, I never mentioned the issue to him again. By the next quarterly meeting, there was a marked improvement in the executive's platform skills and in my own small way, I knew I had made a difference. Beyond the visibility I received, the added by-product of my helping to shore up his weakness was the development of a close working relationship with this executive.

For those employees who believe that the quickest way to attain personal sponsorship is to align themselves with a senior executive, think again. Most of the executives interviewed emphatically believe this strategy to be too risky to one's career. Riding on the coattails of a senior executive, without establishing your own credibility and business track record, results in tremendous vulnerability once that executive leaves the organization—or loses professional credibility. The employee is then left highly exposed and, more often than not, will be forced out of the organization. As one executive bluntly put it, "Those professionals who mirror the style and opinions of the power players without making their own mark are doomed. When the executive goes, they go too!"

Like many of the executives interviewed, I too have seen that very situation occur in a corporation. I worked with an individual who aligned herself with a top executive and even adopted the personality traits of the individual. As the executive was known to be a very combative person, it was no surprise to me that she too began to establish the reputation of being "difficult" by most of the organization. What my colleague failed to realize was that the executive's inherent value and established contribution led most of the organization, including the chairman and CEO, to tolerate his conduct. After the executive retired, my colleague continued to operate in that same combative and arrogant style, and within a very short period of time she was pushed out of the organization.

The lesson illustrated here is that while it is important to actively seek out forums with executives and to be recognized and known within an organization, you will always be better served to first establish yourself as a genuine steward to the corporation. Once that reputation is solidified, all of your interactions with influential people will be based on honest motives, and their opinions will be far more positive about you. In other words, it will be a genuine working relationship rather than a political one.

The Truth About Mentoring

Virtually every executive interviewed talked about how they cultivated relationships with one or several influential people who mentored them throughout the course of their careers. In every instance, the mentoring relationship was fortuitous, one that naturally evolved over the course of time. These relationships developed as influential people observed the employee's performance and gradually sought them out to use their talent. As one executive explained it, "One little thing starts, the person asks you to do something, and then another . . . eventually they begin to invest their time into you on all aspects of the corporation."

Executives are busy people and only have so much time to give to others. It stands to reason that these influential people would be judicious in deciding who receives their time and attention. One executive who has mentored several professionals put it this way: "I guess I just gravitate to those people who strive to do well and work hard."

In an effective mentoring relationship, you receive a wealth of information about the "inner workings" of the organization. The mentor provides you with insights that extend well beyond business strategies and corporate vision. (This often includes, but isn't necessarily limited to, unvarnished assessments of the "players" in the organization.) A true mentor helps the professional develop a better understanding of the corporate culture and political environment of the corporation. At the same time, the mentor provides guidance on how the individual can maneuver through and circumvent those "troubled waters."

As the executives further explained, mentors also serve as valuable sounding boards that an individual can use to share ideas and strategies. The mentor can provide a safe arena for you to test opinions without the fear of reprisal. Other executives commented that simply through "listening and learning," the employee is able to observe the mentor's behavior and then gradually integrate the positive approaches into his or her own persona. In some instances, however, you may observe less desirable behaviors and personality traits demonstrated by the mentor. As one executive explained, "Sometimes you learn from a mentor what *not* to do." As a professional, you may find the personal style of your mentor to be inappropriate or incongruent with your own sense of self. The key is not to simply emulate the mentor—you must develop your own individual style and effectiveness.

Aside from the knowledge and guidance that come from experiencing a successful mentoring relationship, several executives commented on the importance a mentor plays as both lobbyist and champion of one's cause and crusade. One executive described the mentor's influence this way: "Often the mentor serves as the third-party advocate for the employee." As many of the executives further clarified, this advocacy relates to both positive and negative issues encountered by the professional. On the positive front, oftentimes a mentor will help create upward mobility for the individual. One executive shared a personal example, "I had a mentor who was the head of marketing, and when he left the company he influenced the CEO to give me his job."

A handful of executives also shared an interesting benefit provided by mentors that most professionals don't even think about—the "get out of jail free" card. This unspoken truth relates to the inevitable "screw up" that occurs for every professional in his or her career. Virtually every corporate executive will experience a time when a mistake could, and even perhaps should, result in their being severely reprimanded or terminated. In this situation it is often the influential mentor who saves the employee. As one executive recalled, "There were at least two instances when I should have been fired, but because of my mentor, I stayed."

On the other hand, while the majority of executives sang the praises of mentoring relationships, a few of them did share experiences about mentors who demonstrated a more self-serving approach to the relationship. As one executive said, "You have to be careful to ensure that your mentor is looking out for your best interest. I had a mentor who used me to connect to certain 'landmine' situations and in the extreme, breached confidences about information I shared." The point here is that while mentoring programs can serve as internal consulting to professionals, you must enter this nurturing relationship with your eyes wide open. Of course there will be some give and take in the relationship, but if the arrangement becomes more about what you (as the student) can do for the mentor, it is time to move on.

Corporate Matchmaking

Structured mentoring programs excite employees because they believe that these programs will not only provide guidance but also lead to increased visibility within an organization. The truth of the matter, however, is that often these structured matchmaking programs are created more for public relations benefit than for employee success. There are companies who do implement mentoring programs for the right reasons, but in many instances there is little care taken by corporations to effectively create a true mentoring relationship.

The majority of the executives did suggest that structured mentoring programs are effective at providing employees with basic organizational knowledge and core fundamentals about the business. However, in the true definition of an effective mentoring relationship, most believed these structured programs fail to accomplish the objective. One problem with forced mentoring programs stems from the program design itself. An executive shared an example of one company that tried several times to implement a formal mentoring program, but with so many rules that the program failed. "The company designed such a rigid program that it hindered any free exchange between the mentor and the employee. The program just didn't 'take' in the company."

The other reason that structured mentoring programs fail is a result of the individuals selected to be mentors. As one executive succinctly put it, "Just by asking someone to be a mentor doesn't mean you'll get the most fruitful results from that relationship." He further explained that many companies seek out top performers to be mentors, but the most successful professionals are not necessarily adept at coaching others to achieve that same level of performance in an organization. Moreover, such busy individuals may even resent the infringement on their time if they didn't seek to be a part of the program in the first place. Such resentment can then be unintentionally transferred onto the individual they are assigned to mentor.

Close personal working relationships develop over time, and the most significant flaw with forced mentoring is that these programs are inherently artificial. It is unrealistic for a corporation to believe that a program that pairs up two individuals who are unknown to each other will automatically result in an effective mentoring relationship. Like many dating services, this corporate matchmaking may provide a few positive exchanges, but the process rarely leads to a lasting relationship.

From a broader perspective, the other significant problem with structured mentoring programs is in the subliminal message being conveyed, particularly to younger professionals, that the company and the mentor will be responsible for the individual's development and career success. This simply is not the case. Even in the most successful of mentoring programs, the professional might obtain career and performance counseling, but that does not mean that recognition and promotion is guaranteed for the individual.

My advice to professionals who participate in structured mentoring programs is to first be clear about the overall intent of the program. Specifically, I would suggest the actions described in the following sections.

Own the Process

It is important to remember that you yourself are ultimately responsible for your own success. As the recipient of the mentoring program, you must be clear on your own objectives and desires for the program. What are you interested in learning? Who are some of the people in the organization you want to meet? What concerns do you have about the program? Don't delegate your agenda to a mentor who may not want to spend time on your development in the first place.

Get to Know Your Mentor

At the first meeting, spend time learning about the background of your mentor and where he or she fits in the organization. How long has the individual worked for the company? What specific jobs has he held? What was her experience prior to joining the organization? Seek out the commitment level of the mentor by why he or she was interested in being a mentor. How does your mentor view this role?

Understand Everyone's Responsibility

Talk about your goals for the program to ensure that your objectives are clearly aligned with your mentor's. What is the structure of the program? Is there any preparation required before the start of the program? How long does the program last? Does the program require that any supplemental work be completed?

Being prepared and asking important questions will give you greater clarity about the mechanics of the program. It will also establish realistic expectations for all vested parties. More importantly, it will increase the likelihood of achieving a successful mentoring relationship, even in a forced setting.

EXECUTIVESUMMARY

In today's business environment, the truth is that performance in and of itself guarantees nothing for the working professional until people with the power to influence career success recognize that contribution. Given the hundreds, if not thousands, of employees vying for top jobs in most corporations, the cold truth is that visibility and recognition, not hard work, determine career advancement.

While never a deliberate strategy, most of the executives interviewed did confess that they sought out ways to be noticed by influential people. In most cases, however, their active participation was predicated on a genuine desire to broaden their business knowledge rather than seeking the limelight. Even when an executive involved himself in a company-sponsored program, this visibility-seeking approach was a supplemental strategy toward securing a more competitive edge.

It is incredibly naïve, and ultimately self-defeating, to believe that seizing any and all opportunities to "be seen" is a craven political maneuver. As the executives reinforced, if you can step out and differentiate yourself as an individual from the crowd, influential people will tend to provide you with far more opportunities to broaden your knowledge base and skill-sets than the average employee.

However, in order to really distinguish yourself, you must demonstrate exceptional performance and make significant contributions to your organization, rather than simply linking yourself to a highly influential executive. Without establishing some level of a proven track record, seizing opportunities for visibility will prove to be academic. As one executive put it, "Without the substance, executives will simply perceive you as an empty shirt!" ◉

8 | A LACK OF CURIOSITY
KILLS A CAREER

Much attention has been given in recent business literature to the differences and innate value of so-called "A" and "B" players within organizations. "A" players are those 15 percent of employees who radically distinguish themselves from their peers in terms of their performance. They are the high achievers, the rainmakers, the ones who move up the ranks of an organization swiftly and successfully. "B" players, on the other hand, are those employees that, while certainly being competent, don't add extraordinary value to the organization. They perform the duties of their job well, and are even liked and respected within their limited role; however, they never substantially innovate or improve the company's products, processes, or services. While such employees usually have relatively stable job security, they are not those selected for substantial professional or financial advancement.

After ten, twenty, or thirty years in an industry or organization, many such "B" players are often clueless as to why that was the case.

In discussing the issue of employee performance with the executives I interviewed, I asked them to differentiate between the exceptional and the average performer. Although each executive described it differently, there was a common theme. Executives describe the "average performer" as the good, solid person who can be depended on to handle the ordinary tasks. The average person solves the routine problems and is good at projects that are well defined.

Exceptional performers, by contrast, are those individuals who not only address the fundamentals of an issue, but also demonstrate the ability to see all facets of any project or problem. Several of the executives expressed that the exceptional performer tends to have more focus on the broader objectives of the business. As one executive put it, "It's a strategic versus a tactical issue." In short, they see the big picture of how their position, task, or function impacts the organization as a whole.

Regardless of how the executives define performance, all agreed that too many individuals simply do what is asked of them. As one executive expressed, "My frustration with many professionals is that they just don't seem to be as principled—they take too many shortcuts. They don't go through all the steps necessary to ensure that the work product is right or that the problem is thoroughly resolved." In addition, most of the executives confided they have heard every excuse in the book in defense of substandard work. Most employees blame it on a demanding workload or not having enough time, but the end result remains the same: They simply meet the requirements of the job. Failing to take the extra step won't achieve anything but a paycheck and an average performance appraisal.

Beyond the importance of professional curiosity in sustaining one's job, several of the executives also remarked that demonstrating this competency typically leads to far greater visibility for the professional. One executive, for example, shared this specific experience. "When I was just starting out in the sales department, we dealt with packaging issues. I needed and wanted to understand how nylon was made so I asked the individual in charge to explain the process. Unexpectedly, I gained widespread attention because of my interest and curiosity."

Can Curiosity Be Learned?

To begin to understand how to differentiate your own job performance from those around you, we must translate these definitions of average and exceptional performers into specific actions that can be clearly understood and implemented. The key behavior that the executives are describing is what I call "professional curiosity." Professional curiosity may sound simple enough, but it's a far more complicated skill than you might think.

There are two critical requirements of professional curiosity: capacity and drive. Capacity means having the skill or ability to do something, while drive is having the energy and initiative to consistently deliver it. Most people think of a skill as something that is learned. With the executives I interviewed, there were differing opinions on the question "Does everyone have the capacity to be curious?"

While many executives believe that professional curiosity cannot be taught, some, including myself, disagree. For some people, curiosity is innate. You know the type. They were inquisitive as children and have always asked never-ending questions about anything and everything. Others may possess a probing sense about specific areas of interest, while for many, curiosity must be cultivated over time through guidance and experience. Even if you weren't born with natural curiosity, there is still reason to be optimistic. I believe that over time, by experiencing a variety of problems and situations, one can learn how to demonstrate professional curiosity in the workplace.

One executive reinforced his agreement that curiosity can be cultivated based upon his experiences with his own daughters. He shared a story in which he and his wife had given his daughters some money to invest in the stock market. Before they could invest the money, however, they were told that each would have to research and present their proposed investments and rationale behind their choices. One of his daughters, had very little initial curiosity about the stock market. Over time, however, she developed a greater sense of interest about stock prices, financial indicators, and the market.

The executive's story underscores a good point, and one I have seen myself in my many years of executive positions.

Often it is by delving into the details, or developing a broader base of knowledge about your job, organization, or industry, that your job becomes fascinating or compelling. The fact is that even the most exciting industries are filled with mundane positions—particularly if you are a young professional starting out at the bottom of the corporate ladder. Curiosity begets curiosity. By learning more about the company, you become able to add more value to your organization and impress decision-makers within your organization with your energy and verve—a fact that will go a long way toward designating yourself as an "A" player.

Professional Curiosity: Some Practical Examples

Like myself, many of the executives are very familiar with those employees who simply perform the specific tasks of an assignment without applying any conceptual thought to the problem. You'll often hear managers describe this level of performance as "not thinking out of the box." To better illustrate this mediocre behavior and better understand the desired competency of professional curiosity, let's review a practical business application.

A vice president of operations asks a staff analyst to compile a production report for three different product lines: rubber tubing, copper tubing, and steel tubing. The VP adds that he has concerns regarding inefficiencies in the various production lines.

One week later, the analyst returns with the report and informs the VP that the rubber tubing production line is the highest performing line, exceeding the copper production line by 22 percent and the steel production line by 26 percent. The report is well organized and succinct, yet the VP is unhappy with the report. Why?

Let's first discuss what the employee accomplished. Did she indeed provide what was requested? Yes. The VP asked for a production report, and the employee provided it as requested. The problem was that the employee stopped at the data. No analysis or diagnostic thought was conducted to explain "what" the numbers mean or "why" the rubber tubing production was outperforming the other production lines. Consequently, there was no interpretation about whether the production numbers were reasonable, if any of the production lines could be increased, and, if so, how to achieve that goal. Numbers, in and of themselves, are just that—numbers. Executives and key decision-makers look for recommendations to base their decisions upon and action plans to execute those decisions.

The mechanics of simply collecting data is the baseline of performance. The ability to analyze and interpret information is a far more rare and valuable skill, one that requires broader knowledge and conceptual thought. One cannot interpret results or draw conclusions without first diagnosing the problem.

If we were assigning grades, the VP's evaluation of the employee's work would be an "A" for reporting the data and an "F" for analytical and diagnostic skills. The net result would be a "C"—an average mark. While it is true that your work doesn't get returned with letter grades, your boss *does* grade your work. In the corporate world, average won't get you to the top. It just won't. As one executive put it, "It's hard to rely on someone who looks stupid. A person has to be able to present themselves in a way that demonstrates a command of the diagnosis of the problem and the recommended corrective actions."

Even in my own professional experience, I vividly remember trying to explain this very issue to a retail employee. He held the position of merchandise control analyst, a position in which he was responsible for monitoring, analyzing, and reporting the performance of each assigned product group. In his case, it was ladies' sportswear, specifically blouses and sweaters. His responsibility was providing the buyer with each classification's performance. While the employee was successful at the timely reporting of information, the data he reported severely lacked analysis and recommendations for corrective actions—both of which the buyer needed.

I encouraged the analyst to reach conclusions that would assist the buyer in managing the business unit. As I recall, one example was for the classification "long-sleeve sweaters." This classification had been "turning" (or selling) very fast in the stores, yet inventory levels reflected that the buyer should be asking the allocation and distribution departments to accelerate the shipping of merchandise into the stores. The buyer wasn't doing this, yet it stood to reason that the more sweaters in the store, the greater the increase in sales.

As an analyst, it was the employee's job to provide this type of critique. He didn't agree. He said that there were too many classifications to monitor and that it was unrealistic to expect him to make all of these "callouts" with his level of workload. He went on to state that it was unfair to hold him accountable for making recommendations, as he was not the buyer. From his perspective, it was the buyer's responsibility to decide what actions to employ.

Not only did this employee never get to the next level, he ultimately ended up losing his job. Though competent in the baseline requirements of the job, he lost sight of what was most critically needed: interpretation. The plain truth is that competent people are a dime a dozen in today's job market. Companies can find hundreds of people to read numbers and organize them in a spreadsheet, but finding conceptual thinkers who can interpret the data into concrete business terms is a whole different story.

Moreover, while "A" players are always desirable in an organization, there are positions or phases within a company's growth in which an "A" player is a necessity. As illustrated in the previous example, the merchandise control analyst's lack of professional curiosity was adversely impacting the bottom line. The buyer was not accelerating the shipment of additional merchandise into the stores because that recommendation was missing from findings.

Professionals need to be aware that being just a "C" player is not just an impediment to advancement but is sometimes a one-way ticket to the unemployment office. Does your position affect the financials of the organization? Is your company committed to aggressive revenue growth or product development in the short term? Has there been a major change in corporate structure such as an acquisition, a merger, or IPO? If any of those factors are in play at your current place of employment, professional curiosity may be a skill you cannot afford to let slide.

Hopefully these examples better enable you to understand the required actions associated with this label of professional curiosity. That understanding, however, is only half of the battle. While an individual may possess the capacity for being curious, without the drive and desire to consistently demonstrate this ability, nobody can hope to achieve long-term success.

Avoid Intellectual Laziness

Another way of looking at "drive" is to think of it in terms of intellectual laziness.

Reflect on your work performance. It probably isn't difficult for you to distinguish between those assignments where you were truly interested in the work and, as a result, dug deep into the problem, compared to those projects where you had little or no interest and as a result invested only nominal effort. The fact is that deep down, we all know how we are performing at our jobs. We just may not admit it to others or to ourselves.

Think of specific instances in which you went beyond what was asked, thought through the broader ramifications of a decision or proposed action, and made clear, decisive recommendations. Do clear examples come to mind? What about the times when you "skated" through a project just to get it off of your desk? What influenced those choices? Apathy is transparent to everyone, so learn to be aware when you're exhibiting it.

I Have a Plan!

Curiosity is easy enough to describe and understand. For many professionals, however, it is a talent, or competence, that is often difficult to consistently demonstrate at work. The level of output required by corporations is enormous, but the fact still remains that if you are driven to achieve an executive-level position, there are no excuses. Being successful in the corporate world necessitates critical thinking and an inquisitive mindset toward work. My hope is that your passion and interest in business will drive (or at least develop) a greater sense of curiosity about your industry, company, and the work itself.

Still, for many people this ability is not innate. The following sections represent an action plan to assess your own performance and help you immediately demonstrate professional curiosity on the job.

Identify the Problem or Hypotheses

If you do not fully understand the goal of an assignment, ask! Talk to your boss about his hypotheses. Ask him what he is really looking for or hoping to discern from the project.

This step immediately accomplishes two things. It helps your boss see that you are both inquisitive and serious about your work, and it outlines the important issues you need to consider about the project.

You must also understand that on some assignments, your boss may only want the "what" or "why" and not a comprehensive review. You must be able to decipher whether he is looking for the $5 or the $50,000 answer. If you are asking the right questions about the project, you will know the level of diagnosis and "digging in" that is required. If you don't understand something about the assignment, seek clarification. Pretending to know when you don't will almost always result in the delivery of a substandard product.

Develop a Timetable to Allow for Analysis and Interpretation

Whether formal or informal, timelines ensure that work gets done on a timely basis. In committing to due dates for a project, you must allow ample time for both analysis and interpretation. It is easy to provide for the former, but few professionals allow for the latter. Once you have analyzed the data, leave it for a while and then review it with a fresh set of eyes.

The above step may seem to presume that you have all the time in the world to work on assignments. Let's face it. More often than not, that is not the case. Time is money and market share, and professionals must work with a sense of urgency. The good news is that as you practice and improve your professional curiosity, interpretation will eventually become second nature.

Be the Consultant

Think of the assignment as if your boss had come to you as an outside consultant seeking your expertise. This requires that you bring an objective eye and a comprehensive approach to each and every project. As one executive shared, "The people who get ahead figure out what the boss wants before the boss does."

As is the case with any consulting assignment, it may be necessary to collaborate with other departments. Being a good consultant requires that you seek out critical input from those directly or indirectly impacted. You should also seize the opportunity to bounce ideas and hypotheses off your peers. Be careful that you do not operate as a lone wolf, reluctant to share your ideas with peers, or ask advice of others out of a sense of competition. While some colleagues will occasionally steal ideas, be uncooperative, or position themselves at your expense, collaboration is usually more productive, and politically expedient, than competition.

Most importantly, being the consultant does not mean telling your boss what you think he or she wants to hear. While your boss will indeed have beliefs and opinions about the findings on a project, you must submit the results and conclusions in an objective fashion. Otherwise, what is the point of being curious?

Be Succinct and Straightforward

Most executives state that a report comprised of complex language and convoluted thought is the biggest red flag signaling a substandard product. Employees often use this approach as a means of camouflaging their absence of knowledge and business acumen.

If you know what you're talking about, there is no need to make findings complicated. The more succinct you can be, the better. Remember that your assignment is potentially one of hundreds that your boss has to review. The more easily the information is presented, the more impressive the result. Develop the habit of presenting results on one page. Use an outline or bullet points rather than a narrative approach, as it is easier for the decision-makers to read and absorb.

Revisit Your Boss's Goals

Once you have fully analyzed and interpreted the information, go back to your boss's original hypotheses. Have you addressed all of his concerns? Have you raised any additional issues? You may find that additional research and analysis is needed to complete the project. If this happens, talk to your boss right away. Surprising her with additional research and time requirement on the day the project is due puts her in a difficult position—and you in an unfavorable one. Bosses do not like delays or surprises when they are expected to answer to those above them. Being proactive is the key.

EXECUTIVE SUMMARY

We have discussed in detail how professional curiosity greatly influences other people's perception of your performance as average or exceptional, and how being curious will increase the likelihood that you will be considered for promotions. While you don't get to select the assignments you are given, you can control how well you perform those assignments. If achieving a high level of success is indeed your goal, you must consciously decide to demonstrate your professional curiosity with every project and assignment. If you pick and choose when you demonstrate professional curiosity, you run the risk of having your performance evaluated as inconsistent. Inconsistent performance does not result in exceptional performance appraisals or promotions. In other words, demonstrating a lack of professional curiosity kills a career. ◉

9 | DON'T UNDERESTIMATE
THE IMPORTANCE OF ATTITUDE

Most executives will tell you that there is a difference in an organization between being respected and being liked. While more often than not you will hear professionals assert that they'd prefer the former to the latter in the organization, it is important not to underestimate the power of being liked. When I asked the executives to describe to what they attributed their success, more than half commented on their personality, charisma, or ability to ingratiate themselves at all levels in an organization. Distinguishing yourself from others has as much to do with who you are as it does with what you do in the workplace. All things being equal, the employee who proves to be the more likeable individual will advance more swiftly and successfully than the difficult employee.

Indeed, there are many individuals, even senior-level managers, in corporate organizations that engender fear and loathing from peers and subordinates alike. Many of the executives interviewed here cited examples of senior management tolerating difficult behavior from top performers in the organization, primarily because of their significant contribution to the company. Still, the executives also observed that more often than not, that toxic behavior resulted in failure for the top performer somewhere along the course of his or her career. In other words, at some point, sooner or later in their career, these people's bad behavior and lack of likeability *did* catch up with them.

One executive, for example, told me of a situation in which the CEO tolerated the antagonistic behavior of a top-performing colleague because of that individual's outstanding contribution to the organization. However, when the CEO was replaced, the colleague's behavior was unacceptable to the new executive. A short time later, the individual ended up being fired. While being in the good graces of a top executive may enable you to get away with some bad behavior, don't bank on it in the long term. The truth is that if people don't like working with or for you, eventually they will not let your mentor's rank dissuade them from voicing their concerns. Once that executive knows that he or she is endorsing someone the rest of the organization finds distasteful, you will be cut loose. Though the buck may stop with them, smart executives know they can't have dissension in the ranks. Nor do they want employees transferring their dislike of the colleague onto them because they didn't address that person's behavior.

Let's be clear. There is a difference between demonstrating a strong and direct style and behaving in a disruptive, counterproductive, and divisive manner. In talking with each of these executives, I found they consistently demonstrated a definitive and straightforward communication style. At the same time, and perhaps contrary to what many professionals believe, particularly in light of recent corporate scandals such as Enron and Arthur Andersen, the executives also demonstrated a respectful and humanistic concern for both the organization and its employees. As one executive commented, "All too many employees see confidence and kindness as being mutually exclusive. It's a false assumption on their part."

The Likeability Factor

In terms of the likeability factor, once again the caveat for professionals revolves around one's personal motivation. Neither I nor the executives I interviewed suggest feigning pleasantness or concern for others. This false approach is transparent to most people and will quickly be perceived as disingenuous. I recall a time when I held my first real corporate job, working for a senior recruiter. I remember thinking that her upbeat personality seemed a bit too manic to be genuine. One day I observed her berating a subordinate over a very small issue. A few minutes later, the senior vice president of the department passed by, and the recruiter reverted back to her sugary sweet behavior. At twenty-two years of age, if I could see through the Stepford act, it was more than likely that most senior executives would also be able to see through such a phony facade.

In terms of increasing your likeability quotient, the first challenge is to develop a positive mindset toward work in general. As we have discussed, making the right choices about the organization and disciplines in which one works makes that challenge far easier to accomplish. Beyond that behavior, it is also important that a professional treat employees at all levels of the organization with respect and basic human courtesy. The fact is that with all of the time that is spent at the office—and those who harbor ambitions of moving up the corporate ladder usually log in more hours than others—people want to feel some level of personal affiliation with colleagues.

When an individual can capitalize on common interests shared with colleagues, amazing relationships can be cultivated in the long run. For example, in my personal interactions with a senior executive I worked with, I noticed that he was reading a book written by one of my favorite authors. We ended up talking about the book and found that we both shared an interest in mystery novels. The next time the author released a new book, I purchased two copies and forwarded one copy to the executive. My motivation in sending him the book was not to brown nose my way to the top; rather, I simply thought he would enjoy the book. When the executive called to thank me for the gift, we not only shared a nice personal interaction, it also gave me the opportunity to discuss my involvement in a few select projects.

While some professionals might condemn that approach as political, that perspective is immature. Once again, it comes down to the motivation behind the conduct. My motives were genuine. I shared a common interest with the executive and honestly thought he would enjoy the book. However, that also resulted in an opportunity to gain further exposure and, on some level, establish a personal relationship with an influential executive.

As the executives I interviewed consistently reinforced, the ability of professionals to cultivate strong personal relationships with colleagues directly influences their potential for career success. One executive shared an example of a direct report who was complaining about the strained working relationship with a peer in the organization. The executive proceeded to ask his subordinate a few key questions. "How many kids does your peer have? Do they play soccer? What does your peer do in his spare time?" To no surprise of the executive, his employee had no idea. This executive then went on to explain to the individual that his inability to establish a personal connection with the problem peer might be part of the trouble. As he put it, "Essentially, there was no relationship, personal or otherwise, between this employee and his colleague." That lack of personal interaction had derailed the working relationship.

Attitude Makes or Breaks a Career

Those who operate in a "head down" fashion, focusing solely on the work without cultivating healthy relationships, not only limit their exposure to key players in the company, but also stifle any chance to build camaraderie and collaboration at any level in an organization. I draw the analogy to the straight "A" college student who devotes no time to any extracurricular activities. Spend any time with some of those individuals, and you often find that while they may be brilliant, they are not always very interesting to be around. The same principle holds true at work. Being the brightest, but socially inept, does not typically lead to achieving high levels of success in the corporate world.

The most common attitudinal issues conveyed by the executives typically fell into the following three categories.

The "No-Can-Do" Person

As the label implies, the no-can-do individual always has a problem accepting new assignments, complains about being overworked, and is unwilling to assist colleagues in any way. The professional, and I use the term loosely, focuses solely on the work directly linked to his position and responds negatively to any unexpected deviation from his routine. This attitude is particularly frustrating to managers during periods of tight time constraints. The no-can-do person rarely, if ever, demonstrates the willingness to assist in a crisis. Worse still is that even when the person actually agrees to help out on a project, the personal griping that often accompanies the effort negates any contribution made by the individual on the assignment.

It is important to note that all it takes are a few instances of negativity and "no" responses for you to be identified by managers as a problem. People quickly begin to work around the "no" individual. Ultimately this negative behavior hinders career potential, and it also often leads to dismissal. Several of the executives made this interesting observation. Often, the average performer who demonstrates a "can do" attitude is far more valued in the organization than the more competent employee who is less of a team player. As one executive put it, "I have seen really capable people fail simply because they were a constant negative force."

Functioning as a corporate "roadblock" not only proves frustrating to superiors but also to one's peers. In talking about their own success, most executives commented that they worked very hard to establish collaborative relationships with their peers. Even to this day, each assists colleagues with problems and provides genuine support to their departmental initiatives. Several executives also shared the opinion that all too many professionals focus on upward communication and attitude with little care or concern for peer relations. As one executive commented, "Being cooperative and being competitive are not mutually exclusive in the working world." Some professionals embrace the mindset that building cohesive relationships with peers somehow jeopardizes their competitive edge; they truly do not understand the importance of cross-functional support. As one executive shared, "Your peers can make or break you in the corporate world. No one works in a vacuum."

The other reason the "no" individual will be stifled in his career potential is that executives do not want that attitude being imparted to subordinates. No executive in his right mind would put such a negative force into a supervisory role, where it would create an entire department of "no" people running around the corporation. Even when the professional produces such exceptional results that the organization still values the individual, the best-case scenario is that the "no" person will be able to continue to perform in an individual contributor role, with no chance for promotion.

The easiest way to gain recognition and differentiate yourself from the rest of the corporate population is to be identified as the "go to" person. Demonstrating an attitude of receptivity to any and all work assignments, regardless of the effort required, will serve you well throughout your career.

The "Personal Problem" Child

How many times have you worked with a colleague who constantly discussed his or her personal problems in the workplace? My guess is too many times to count. While everyone experiences difficulties in their personal lives, the truth is that no one at work really wants to hear about them.

There is nothing more frustrating than having to manage an employee who is in a bad mood because of problems in his personal life. That is not to say that there aren't colleagues and managers who won't listen to your problems or lend a sympathetic ear, but the truth is that the work must still get done. In fact, many executives articulated situations when it is important to provide an employee with the forum to vent their frustrations. The harsh reality, however, is that most managers simply do not have the time. The other danger is that if colleagues perceive you as not being able to manage your personal life, they will eventually conclude that you can't manage your professional life. That may sound cold or unfair, but when managers hear an employee whose job description involves delivering revenue lament about their credit card debt, or a peer whose position entails sensitive negotiations talk about how "burned out" they are, it gives them a crisis of confidence in that employee.

More often than not, managers oversee a large group of employees. If one stands out as having constant personal problems, I guarantee that the employee's days are numbered. As one executive bluntly put it, "If the person becomes too disruptive to the group, they have to go." Any professional who talks incessantly about his problems and interferes with the harmony of the department will quickly find himself in either a counseling session or on the receiving end of a corrective action.

Even if one's manager is tolerant of such issues, the other danger for the individual is that the behavior will interfere with work performance. It stands to reason that it would be difficult to achieve an acceptable level of performance when personal matters are so distracting from duties and responsibilities. It is important to remember that your company pays its employees in return for a desired level of contribution. Simply put, do your job! Take care of your personal business on your own time, and keep your problems to yourself.

At the same time, the truth is that most managers have experienced some level of either personal or family difficulties at some point in their careers. As a result, most of them are more than willing to make *short-term* accommodations for employees. It is only when the exception becomes the rule that most managers will begin to take issue with the behavior.

In those truly exceptional cases when a significant personal issue may adversely impact your effort or performance, my advice is to proactively discuss the matter with your boss. For example, I managed an individual who worked very long hours and produced a tremendous amount of work. He never complained about the late nights or the demands of his job, but one day he came to see me about a personal problem. He explained that his wife was going through some difficult issues and was giving him a hard time about his work hours. He asked if he could temporarily reduce his hours to accommodate being home with his wife in the evenings. I told the employee to take whatever time he needed to be with his wife and reinforced that if he needed me to redistribute his work to others in the department, I'd be happy to do so.

The accommodation lasted about a month, during which time he would leave by 5:30 P.M. while still managing to contribute in a significant way. Ultimately, he resumed his normal pace and performance level. As the example illustrates, in these rare cases you will usually find your manager to be far more understanding and willing to accommodate your needs if you are proactive, discreet, and work to minimize the impact of your personal issue on the company as much as possible.

The "Chip-on-the-Shoulder" Professional

Unlike the aforementioned attitudinal issues, the chip-on-the-shoulder professional typically performs at a very high level and produces above-average results. As described by many of the executives, this employee type is usually a younger professional who achieves a few wins on the job and then suddenly becomes the arrogant, all-knowing employee. As one executive described this profile, "The arrogant ones are those who actually believe that they know more than everyone else . . . and it shows!" Another executive bluntly defined the behavior this way: "It's the guy who starts to believe his own bullshit."

The specific behaviors that the executives often associate with this individual include the following:

- Poor listening skills—Quick to interrupt colleagues while they are speaking; insensitive and impatient to others' approach to problem-solving or the time required to process information.
- Nonverbal cues—Visually showing disapproval or dis-agreement with a shared opinion (rolling the eyes or shaking of the head).
- Domineering attitude toward colleagues—Presents ideas with a "my way is the best way" approach; behav-ior indicates infatuation with sound of own voice.

The good news for the arrogant professional is that most executives are far more willing to allow this behavior than the other two attitudinal issues already discussed. In my own experience as a senior-level executive, it has never ceased to amaze me how tolerant other executives are of this behavior from top performers. This is so true that corporations often end up creating their own monsters. As a result, the chip-on-the-shoulder professional is often consumed by the desire to impress superiors and sees no merit in cultivating peer relationships.

However, if you fall into this attitudinal pattern, be warned. The potential for disaster exists when your behavior begins to create strained relationships with peers—which, be assured, it eventually will. When a professional demonstrates arrogant behavior over an extended period of time, he or she will also begin to get isolated. Furthermore, the individual is likely to encounter a lack of cooperation or even sabotage from colleagues. As one executive remarked, "Peers don't get mad—they get even." The ability to accomplish significant results in the corporate world often requires a more flexible and compromising style than is typically demonstrated by this behavioral profile. It is often that rigidity that leads to failure. As one executive commented, "The ones that come with the big egos, before they've earned it, typically fail because they didn't know how to be conciliatory."

Aside from professional coaching as a means of correcting the behavior, failure is usually the only catalyst for change in an arrogant individual. A severe professional setback will typically serve to humble the individual and knock them back into the realities of corporate life.

EXECUTIVE SUMMARY

Too many professionals focus on developing their technical expertise and furthering their education, devoting years to mastering a profession, only to limit their possibilities because they simply cannot get along with other people. Whether it's arrogance, ego, or the lack of social graces that are to blame, managers truly don't care. They are less inclined to believe that these deficiencies can be coached to improvement. The cold hard truth is that without the ability to demonstrate expected behaviors in a corporation, even the most competent professional will remain hindered in terms of career growth. Worse yet, such attitudinal issues may jeopardize, or terminate, a career altogether. ☉

10 | THE LOST ART OF HONORING YOUR COMMITMENTS

Today's technological gadgets—e-mail, PDAs, beepers, and cell phones—were all developed to increase response time, yet it can still take several weeks to get a call returned! Have we created a world of decreased expectations about service and commitment? According to most of the executives surveyed, the answer is a resounding "Yes!" As one executive put it, "When it comes to responsiveness, what used to be the norm is now the exception to the rule."

The majority of executives I interviewed were appalled by the lack of responsiveness demonstrated by the working world. Like me, most grew up in corporate cultures that instilled the importance of keeping one's word and of being responsive to the needs of the organization. I remember being taught to respond to any phone call within twenty-four hours. Furthermore, managers conveyed that the twenty-four-hour expectation was nonnegotiable!

No matter what it took, employees returned every call within the established time frame.

The fact of the matter is that some employees simply do not see the value of fulfilling commitments. They find it difficult to distinguish between important issues and the mundane. In addition, too many professionals lose sight of the importance of serving the needs of their bosses. Even when furthering your own ambitions, making your boss happy is rule number one in the working world. According to the majority of executives, the stellar performers always tend to their boss's needs and requests. As one executive remarked, "It's rule number one   take care of your boss. You'd be surprised, but people forget."

On a more global basis, several executives defended their own organizations, stating that their culture promotes the importance of commitment and responsiveness. Many of these same executives, however, went on to say many employees perceive these values as being inefficient. What was most interesting was that executives tended to assess those professionals who didn't see the value of responsiveness as average or below-average performers. In describing the commitment of top performers, executives described exceptional performers as those who always deliver projects on time and are highly responsive to all levels of the organization. The top performer never has to be reminded about deadlines, nor do you ever hear about them failing to respond to a phone call or e-mail. "My top performers always deliver . . . even before the project is due. It's the average guys you have to be worried about."

Technology—Tool or Trap?

While the executives appreciate the immediacy of information provided by the advent of technological tools, they also view these mechanisms as a trap for most corporate professionals. The executives asserted that the problem with these information tools revolves around their misuse by professionals in the workplace. Many executives felt that younger professionals become too consumed with a "more is better" approach. One executive commented that these gadgets have become the new status symbol for most of the younger professionals. He provided an example involving one of his attorneys who approached him with a request for a specific type of PDA. When he inquired about the need for the new gadget, she commented that one of her peers had received one, and as they both were at the same level in the organization she thought it only appropriate that she have one too. Needless to say, the executive was shocked by the employee's rationale. This example clearly illustrates how this ever-changing technology can cause too many employees to focus on superficial issues rather than their own responsiveness to the needs of the business.

One of the interesting contradictions discussed by executives was that while technology makes the availability of critical data far more accessible, it often creates a "title wave" of information that becomes overwhelming for professionals and requires far too much time in which to respond. Executives shared numerous frustrations regarding electronic communication in the workplace. They cited plenty of examples in which their staff exercised a "more is better" approach to communication, inundating the executive with too much unnecessary information.

One particularly interesting comment shared by many of the executives revolved around their approach to managing e-mails. Many explained that if the important information was not contained within the first few sentences, they simply deleted the message. Undoubtedly, many employees will be mortified to hear that remark, after having spent hours on preparing the all-too-comprehensive electronic message designed to impress the boss. The important message to professionals is simple—be brief in your electronic correspondence, and get to the point of the matter. Executives are extremely pressed for time, and they don't want information for information's sake. They look for employees who can cull data into a few pertinent facts—and those who respect their time. Don't think you're gaining their respect by e-mailing them every fifteen minutes.

In fact, many of the executives expressed that in many instances, they would actually prefer a conversation to an e-mail. Executives are of the opinion that too many professionals hide behind the computer, to avoid difficult conversations rather than confronting issues in a face-to-face manner. What employees often fail to recognize is that the use of e-mail as a primary communication tool hinders them from developing strong working relationships with influential leaders. The executives reinforced the need for professionals to develop a more balanced approach to corporate communication.

Even when they do get to speak to someone on the telephone, executives comment that often the individual is talking and "clicking" all at the same time. As one executive commented, "They are typing away on the computer, and they're not fully engaged in the conversation. It makes me mad because I feel like I am not being respected."

Personal Agendas Versus Company Responsibilities

While on the one hand executives attribute a professional's lack of responsiveness to being overwhelmed with information, many also believe that in some cases it is a result of individuals believing their own self-importance. As one executive conveyed, "I believe that in general, many people in leadership positions in corporate America have forgotten their responsibilities. Many have let their personal agendas take priority over their commitment and responsiveness to the shareholders."

I encountered one of these "all too important" professionals myself while conducting my research for this book. One executive agreed to have a preliminary phone conversation with me to discuss the overview of the book and the nature of the interview process. As he maintained a rather hectic schedule, his executive assistant actually had to schedule the fifteen-minute phone call several weeks in advance. On the day of the scheduled interview, the executive assistant informed me that due to the executive's "demanding" schedule we would have to reschedule the appointment. Understanding that executives indeed are extraordinarily busy, I gladly rescheduled the phone call. Long story short, after the third call to reschedule the appointment, I graciously explained to the assistant that I was no longer interested in rescheduling the discussion. I asked her to explain to the executive that in experiencing such difficulty in orchestrating a fifteen-minute call, I had little or no confidence in his ability to commit to a two-hour interview. In addition, I also conveyed that I viewed his behavior as incredibly disrespectful both of my time and to me personally. It should come as no surprise to know that I never received a follow-up phone call from the executive.

Many executives admit that they too have observed similar conduct from other executives who simply allow their own personal agendas or egos to interfere with their responsibility to provide service and value to the corporation's internal and external customers and shareholders. Several executives went on to say that this self-absorbed behavior sends the wrong message to the rest of the organization. The reality is that when many corporate executives expound upon the importance of responsiveness and keeping one's word, it is more a case of "Do as I say, not as I do." One example that illustrated this point came from an executive whose staff was responsible for developing and conducting corporate diversity training sessions that were mandatory for all employees to attend. Shortly after the meetings began, his staff began to complain about several executives who had either cancelled their attendance at the last minute or were a no-show. As the executive remarked, "The message being sent by these executives is that mandatory only applies to lower levels in the company."

EXECUTIVESUMMARY

Values such as integrity and credibility are still given credence by leaders in today's corporations. Regardless of the corporate culture or the demonstrated behavior of an organization's leaders, professionals need only concern themselves with demonstrating a high level of responsiveness and consistently delivering on their commitments. The good news is that when you honor your commitments and deliver results on time or ahead of schedule, you can quickly gain the attention of others and build an immediate reputation of credibility. True, in and of itself, this behavior won't get you to the top, but demonstrating these high standards will quickly lead to increased visibility and recognition by those individuals who influence your career opportunities. ◉

I took my first position in corporate America at the age of twenty. As a human resources professional, I interacted with a variety of executives and showed them the utmost respect and courtesy. It was always my expectation that as I gradually proved myself, my discussions with them would progress beyond pleasantries and perfunctory exchanges to more strategic-level discussions about company policy. However, if anyone had ever told me that I would be invited to attend an executive meeting so early in my tenure with the company, I would have thought they were crazy. Within my first year, however, I was provided a bird's-eye view of the executive wing.

While assigned to recruit production workers during an attempt to form a union at my company's food manufacturing plant, I was invited to participate in a meeting to discuss the reasons that the employees in the plant were attempting to unionize. There I was in the executive boardroom, the youngest person in the room, not to mention the only female. I was incredibly nervous, yet I was also exhilarated by the exposure and opportunity to sit in with the top executives. My senior vice president took great care to introduce me to every "suit" in the room, which included the CEO of the company. One gentleman I met, an outside consultant, referred to me as the "mole" of the division. In my naïveté, I did not understand the comment and certainly wasn't offended by it, but my SVP quickly took him to task on the remark. I vividly remember being impressed by my boss's courage in speaking his mind, and it proved to be a valuable and timely lesson for me.

As the meeting progressed, the same outside consultant waxed on about the pivotal issues causing the employees to attempt unionization. He cited health benefits and wages as the employee's primary concerns, and then proposed an immediate resolution strategy.

As I listened, his comments seemed incongruent with my own experiences and observations of the division. Having spent a significant period of time working side by side with the employees, I believed his opinions were incorrect. However, who was I to say that my opinions were right and his were wrong? I was a young, inexperienced professional with far less insight than this senior consultant. I continued to listen quietly when suddenly, without thinking, I found myself speaking up. I explained to the group of executives that during my time in the division, I found the frustrations of the employees to be far less complicated than benefits and wages. I described the poor working conditions of the facility, and the employees' impression that management didn't care about the employees.

As I continued, I wasn't aware that in sharing my opinions I was directly contradicting the opinion of the consultant. I could see on his face that he was irritated. When I finished, he attempted to dismiss my findings as an oversimplification of the situation. My heart started to race and I could feel myself flushed in embarrassment. To my surprise, however, the CEO calmly explained that there was no reason why the organization could not address all issues in an attempt to quash the union attempt. Afterwards, my SVP praised me for my contribution to the meeting and told me I had handled myself very professionally. The CEO, calling me by name, thanked me for my effort in the division and for my insight. Score one for the youngster!

That experience was invaluable. It taught me that it is the responsibility of every professional, a fiduciary duty if you will, to share honest and candid opinions regarding issues critical to the business. Be aware, however, that this honest feedback all comes down to one's personal motivation. Candor should be used to convey issues that are important to the business—not for grandstanding or personal recognition. It was not my intent to discredit or embarrass the consultant; rather, I had genuine concern for the well being of the employees and in providing the senior management team with honest insight into the situation.

Don't Avoid Controversy—Create It!

Most of the executives I interviewed had also learned the same lesson early on about the value of speaking their mind or sharing a contrary opinion. Interestingly enough, a handful of the executives commented that they actually seek out opportunities to create controversy with colleagues. As one executive crudely put it, "I enjoy teeing up shit storms." Their belief is that by creating controversy, you force colleagues to think more creatively—and often this approach results in better ideas and broader problem-solving techniques. They further dispelled the common misconception that controversy breeds a zero-sum game or a win/lose scenario. In their own experiences, creative conflict typically leads to greater compromise by the vested parties.

Several executives further reinforced the importance of knowing the difference between a battle and the war. A professional may not win a particular argument, but he or she may indeed still successfully influence the outcome. As one executive stated, "I may take on a battle, but it doesn't mean I am going to win. What I learned, though, is that sometimes you change someone's mind in the process."

Get Beyond the Fear

When I asked the executives why they believed that all too many professionals were reluctant to speak out on issues, most thought that people were afraid of being embarrassed by others or "beaten up" for sharing a contrary opinion. While many executives admitted that they too were nervous about sharing a contrary position, the needs of the organization and its employees far outweigh any trepidation they may have about creating internal conflict.

Several of the executives provided examples that illustrated the importance of setting one's personal feelings and fears aside for the greater good of the organization. One male executive put it this way: "If I'm in conflict with one of my comrades over an issue and it's important to the 5,000 employees in my organization, you can bet that I'm going to fight until I win. My employees are worth it." One of the female executives also shared an example when she sat in a meeting with her hands shaking because she knew she was going to have her head handed to her by her boss. As she commented, "It was worth it to me because it was the right thing to do for the company."

From my conversations with these individuals, who sit in *Fortune* 500's most senior-level jobs, it became apparent that they possessed far greater professional self-confidence than the majority of people working in the corporate world. By their own admission, these successful leaders have developed a thicker skin in the face of adversity, as their primary goal is to significantly influence the bottom-line performance of their corporations rather than exercising their own personal power. They are living proof that a true sense of self and professional self-confidence not only influence your ability to openly express opinions, but are qualities genuinely valued by most corporations.

As one executive commented, "You have to know who you are and have the conviction to stand behind your beliefs. Otherwise you're always going to be afraid and will cower when confronted or challenged by others on your ideas. What you find is that while many executives won't necessarily like your approach, they do respect opinions that add value to the company."

Watershed Moments

While it is one thing for professionals to know that in sharing contrary opinions they are contributing to the greater good of a corporation, the experience itself can prove to be quite unsettling. Many of the executives still recall their own watershed moments, when in sharing a contrary opinion they were aggressively confronted by an influential executive. The first time a professional encounters such a difficult experience, the situation often serves as a personal crossroads or turning point. You must decide what you stand for and what risks you are willing to take in honestly speaking your mind about an issue. In my own experience, I've seen many professionals retreat from the challenge. They are so afraid of contradicting their bosses, and possibly jeopardizing their careers, that they play it safe and only offer shallow observations designed to offend no one.

The problem is that in order to have substantial professional advancement and to serve the organization you work for, you must be willing to get in up to your waist. No one will respect you if you don't. It is important to remember that at the executive level, the issues and decisions have far-reaching effects. As such, the needs of the corporation dictate that the players sitting in these jobs be willing to confront and debate ideas and decisions to serve as genuine stewards to their stakeholders.

My own personal watershed moment in my career occurred when the president of my company asked me to share my thoughts on a decision proposed by his direct report, a senior vice president of operations. Although I knew that my opinion was contrary to that of his protégé, I took a deep breath and reluctantly told the truth. What followed was a scathing tongue-lashing about my audacity to contradict the decision of a more senior executive. With my heart pounding and visions of my career coming to a fatal end, I found myself responding, "If you didn't want my opinion then why did you ask for it in the first place?" Surprisingly, this brought the executive to an immediate halt. I wasn't sure what the silence meant, but I knew that if I was going to lose my job over the matter, I wanted to go out with my integrity intact.

Interestingly enough, I didn't lose my job. I received more frequent visits from the president, and we developed a much closer relationship. In fact, he became one of my biggest supporters in the corporation. In retrospect, what I perceived to be a personal attack from the president actually turned out to be his way of testing my own personal conviction. My experience highlights an important point that every professional must understand—a challenge by an individual does not necessarily mean disagreement or disapproval. Oftentimes a superior's combative approach is simply a means of ferreting out whether you are a corporate blowhard or a true professional who can stand firm in your opinions. If you can pass the test, more than likely, you won't have to endure it again from that particular individual.

Getting Past Differences in Style

One of the difficulties in speaking your mind is being confronted by colleagues or superiors whose style is highly combative and hostile. The executives I interviewed explained that often, antagonistic behavior is a result of a specific corporate culture. As one executive shared, "My style was directly influenced by the corporate culture I grew up in—that culture promoted a very aggressive, forceful, and direct style. In that world, if you were more reserved, people would roll right over you."

Some executives also commented that personal style might be a function of the individual's role in an organization. As one executive clarified, "There has to be an ability to look at it from the other person's perspective. CFOs tend to be very intimidating, but if my job was to say 'No' to everybody, I'd probably develop that style too." The individual went on to say, "In corporations today, it is often difficult to maintain one's own sense of style because there is pressure to conform to a model."

When asked how a professional can effectively manage communication in a corporate culture that is contrary to their own personal style, several of the executives quickly responded, "You either adapt or you get out."

In my own professional experience, I too found this advice to be true. I worked in a corporation that promoted a very aggressive and confrontational approach to communication. I observed a peer's career become stifled because she was too soft-spoken and could not confront colleagues in the manner that the culture deemed effective. As time went on, it became clear that she would never achieve an officer-level position, even though she was extremely competent. Ultimately, my colleague left the organization and joined a company whose culture was more congruent with her own beliefs and attitudes.

The difficulty with the "jumping ship" approach, however, is that there are no guarantees that the new corporation is going to be any different from the previous one. In fact, most executives believe that at some point in any professional's career, they will be confronted with difficult or antagonistic personalities. When encountering a hostile personality (particularly a superior), professionals all too often become paralyzed by the confrontation and lose all footing on the issue at hand. As a result, they become unable to articulate an opinion or position and are quickly overshadowed by the dominant personality. For those professionals who are committed to working through a particular culture, the challenge then becomes identifying ways to effectively communicate their opinions while maintaining their own authentic style.

Focus on the Facts

The executives spoke at length about the importance of effectively expressing opinions and ideas. However, more emphasis was placed on the substance of the opinion being conveyed than on the manner in which opinions are shared. In fact, the majority of executives commented that they communicate far more effectively by presenting logic and data in support of their opinions rather than "jumping up and down" or "pounding fists on the desk."

Particularly when there are stylistic differences, a professional will always be better served by staying focused on the relevant business issues, and his or her own knowledge, and not becoming distracted by personal style issues. When you become preoccupied with approach and delivery, rather than supporting opinions, reason, and data, you risk getting labeled as a bully and losing all credibility amongst your peers and superiors.

In those cases when an extremely volatile or emotionally charged individual aggressively confronts you, as a professional, you may have to demonstrate a more forceful approach to send a clear message to the "wild one." As one executive put it, "Sometimes difficult people have to learn that they can't push you around." Another executive shared an example in which her boss was berating another colleague in such an abusive manner that she actually walked out of the meeting. Interestingly enough, the leader later apologized for his conduct.

When you are confronted with difficult personalities, the executives I interviewed advised that you maintain your composure and concentrate on the matters at hand. Once employees allow themselves to become intimidated and distracted from the critical issues, they too often are unable to clearly communicate their opinions and ultimately will appear unprepared or ineffective.

Five Keys to Speaking Up Effectively

While conceptually it is easy to understand the importance of candor in the workplace, the harsh reality is that speaking up is easier said than done. In seeking advice about speaking one's mind, the executives shared the following strategies for improving communication and garnering respect from others in an organization.

Speak the Truth

It was good advice when you were a kid, and it still holds true in the corporate world. No organization is well served by only hearing the popular opinion. In fact, most executives disdain "yes" people. As one executive expressed, "There should be no surprises. I always speak the truth as I see it . . . that's what I get paid to do." If the culture of the organization does not value the truth, perhaps it's time to find a new organization.

Be Clear on Your Position

It is important to convey your opinions in a way that is easily understood and targets the appropriate audience. As one executive commented, "If you give me a presentation and I can't understand it, I'll tell you to get out! People are so caught up with acronyms that they simply cannot communicate well." While you want to simplify your message and be as succinct as possible, never dumb down the content.

Don't Make It a Personal Issue

Remember that your goal is to support the success of the corporation rather than your own personal agenda. While you may encounter individuals who approach the discussion as a personal competition, don't play the same game.

It is also important to understand that often the opinions or position of an individual are not personally motivated; rather, they are simply approaching the issue in a different way. As one executive shared, "I have learned that when I assumed it was a personal issue, the person was just coming at it from a different perspective."

Maintain Your Professional Conviction

Regardless of the push-back you may receive from colleagues and superiors, remain focused on your position. If you allow yourself to waiver on your opinions, you may be perceived as lacking either the confidence or the expertise required for making critical decisions—and organizations don't promote people who can't make decisions. Also, management positions often require advocacy. That might mean sticking up for your company's service or product to clients and vendors; getting more resources for your division; or defending strategic initiatives to a board or stockholders. If you can't maintain your professional convictions, you won't be an effective advocate for your organization.

Consider All Points of View

While you should maintain conviction in your ideas and beliefs, you can also gain respect by modifying your ideas after considering all points of view. Show some flexibility! Remember, it isn't about winning and losing. Instead, the goal is to arrive at the best solution to the problem. As one executive put it, "Oftentimes, the best solution involves a compromise."

EXECUTIVE SUMMARY

When you're just starting out in an organization, it is often very scary to stand up and say, "I don't agree," particularly when the individuals on the receiving end do not want to hear it. Being successful in the corporate world requires you to take some risks, and that means sometimes getting "knocked around" when your opinion is contrary to that of influential leaders. That said, however, virtually all of the executives perceived their ability to share the undesired idea or opinion as their duty and obligation to the employees and shareholders of the corporation.

Being an honest broker in an organization does not mean that every disagreement or heated debate result in fisticuffs. The key is to cultivate a professional style that expresses thoughts and ideas in a manner that is congruent with the corporate culture. If you find, however, that the environment promotes a communication style that conflicts with your personal values, then it is time to consider a change of company. Life is too short to wear corporate masks and sustain an unnatural façade for the sake of your success.

The cold hard truth is that if you approach your career as a popularity contest, your success will never find its way to the fast track. You'll muddle through a series of jobs and perhaps achieve a modicum of success but will never hold the most influential positions in a corporation. ◉

12 | MAKING YOURSELF INDISPENSABLE

It's an undeniable fact that today's corporate environment is much more dispassionate than it was forty, thirty, or even twenty years ago. Corporations used to adopt a paternal approach to managing their employees, which was reflected in generous pension plans, a steady promotion track (largely) based on tenure, and lifelong employment—provided you didn't colossally screw up.

Today everyone in the working world can be replaced. Indispensability is no longer predicated on skills, loyalty, rank, or even competent performance. Most companies, however, protect those performers who demonstrate the most significant value to the corporation. In asking the executives their opinions on the matter, most emphatically agreed with the notion that one can indeed supply "indispensability" to an organization.

Senior management does identify top performers who, under adverse circumstances, will always be ensured a position—those are the "A" players, discussed in Chapter 8. Even in workforce reductions or consolidations, the "chosen ones" will always be protected from job loss, even if it requires that the individual be moved to another position in the company.

Corporations identify their top performers through both formal and informal methods. It is a common formalized practice for managers to "force rank" their employees, listing each staff member in descending order, based upon overall performance. This process not only takes into consideration an employee's individual contribution, it also factors in the perceived "added value" that the individual provides to the corporation. This value could include the employee's breadth of knowledge, scope of responsibility, or the specific business expertise that he or she possesses. Once this data is compiled at a departmental level, the functional leaders and divisional vice presidents then perform the same process, until the most senior officers in the organization have compiled one consolidated list of the company's most valuable core of professionals.

While this premeditated separation of wheat from the chaff may surprise some professionals and sound unbelievably calculated, it is a fact of corporate life. Your objective should be to figure out how to identify yourself as part of this select group of employees. The art of making yourself indispensable to an organization can be accomplished in three primary ways:

- Mastering your primary area of knowledge.
- Creating a niche in your business.
- Expanding your area of responsibility.

Although each executive I interviewed ranked these steps in various orders of importance, every one of them agreed that all of the approaches directly influence indispensability to a corporation. It is important to note that you do not have to achieve all three objectives to be deemed as highly valued to senior executives. However, if you want to increase your potential for success, you should focus on achieving all the steps. The process of selecting the most highly regarded employees is a highly competitive one. To achieve such recognition, you must demonstrate a far broader value to the organization.

Mastering Your Primary Area of Knowledge

In the simplest of terms, mastering your primary area of knowledge requires that you develop and demonstrate a comprehensive knowledge and competence in your chosen discipline. Beyond your ability to handle everyday tasks or routine assignments, this means being equipped to address more strategic issues and undertake the more complex problems of the department.

This method also speaks to the way in which you as a professional approach your job. An indispensable performer is never complacent and is constantly seeking out new ways to improve his or her position. One executive described it this way: "The master will redefine their role, give it new texture and deliver results that are unexpected by the organization." As the executives further reinforced, ultimately, exceptional performers establish themselves as true change agents for the function.

As the executives explained, one of the easiest ways for professionals to demonstrate their expertise is by actively addressing and correcting critical problems in their area. One executive shared the example of being transferred into a position that many thought was a "nowhere" job. He was responsible for managing a group of attorneys and overseeing the litigation process. Although the executive was concerned that this position could potentially sideline him from becoming general counsel, he still approached the position with the same interest and commitment that he had demonstrated in his previous roles. He quickly identified significant issues in the department and used his knowledge and expertise to correct the problems. He initiated the development of an automated litigation management system and personally created a training program that taught attorneys how to effectively manage outside counsel. These programs not only improved inefficiencies but positively influenced expense controls for the function. The results achieved by the executive were quickly recognized by senior leaders and led to further promotions throughout his career.

Solving the Key Problems

Beyond demonstrating competency in your area of responsibility, most executives agree that there is another way you can improve your perceived value: Apply your knowledge and skill to core businesses and the strategic direction of the company. In one position that an executive held early on in his career, he identified the need to develop improved tracking of operational results for the company. He took the initiative to obtain all of the information from more than 300 districts and then manually compiled the data into organized reports. In addition to consolidated reporting, the executive then developed critical performance measures and standards to be used in performance evaluations. Not only did the CEO love the recommendations, the process became the corporate model for tracking and managing business results.

Another executive related his own personal experience with adding value to a corporation. While functioning as a chief trial attorney, he was asked by senior management to oversee the trial of a class action discrimination lawsuit that had potentially significant financial implications for the corporation. While the attorneys representing the company were of the mindset to fight the suit to the bitter end, this executive quickly determined that there was indeed culpability with regard to the company's actions alleged in the case. He quickly intervened and successfully settled the matter for far less money than the corporation might have paid in judgments awarded in the case. Beyond the settlement, this executive proposed changes to existing management practices to prevent any future litigation. As a result of his performance, senior management began to refer to the executive as the "fix it" guy.

Creating a Niche

The term "niche" is most often used to refer to individual business products or services that differentiate a corporation from its competitors in a particular segment of the marketplace. The workplace itself, however, also provides a professional with the opportunity to establish a personal niche. A personal niche would be a specific knowledge or competency a professional possessed that not only delivered significant value but was also very difficult to replicate or replace in the corporation.

It is important to understand that the ability to establish a niche correlates to your expertise. One executive asserted that as professionals encounter a variety of experiences over the course of their careers, they build up an "intellectual reservoir" that is highly valued by an organization. He cited an example of when he and several staff members handled the negotiation process on their first labor contract. He commented that while the experience was incredibly difficult for the group members, they began to develop successful negotiation skills and tactics. With every subsequent contract, the group performed at even higher levels as a result of their previous experience at the bargaining table. Over time, the team established itself as the labor negotiation experts and became indispensable to the corporation.

Executives shared numerous examples involving employees who were highly regarded because of the niche they had created in their organizations. One executive described the performance of such an individual, calling him the "one-man band" for the marketing department. This employee had established himself as the guru at developing critical tools that dramatically improved the performance of the sales force. The executive further commented that the other reason the employee was so invaluable to the company was that he was genuinely interested in improving the business. Not surprisingly, this executive remarked that she is constantly bombarded with requests from colleagues seeking the employee's assistance on a variety of critical projects.

While creating a niche can lead to indispensability, a number of executives caution professionals to remain focused on their long-term career opportunities. Their contention is that often a niche can be so highly valued by an organization that the professional runs the risk of becoming a victim of his own success. You may become so skilled in an area that leaders are reluctant to move you into another area, meaning you end up pigeonholed. The trick is to seize opportunities to fill a unique and valuable need in the organization while maintaining focus on your overall career objectives. Solicit additional projects while serving in the highly valued role. If you can demonstrate the ability to manage multiple projects and function in the niche, the less likely you are to be typecast. As a result of your broadened performance, the organization will have a vested interest in tending to your career in the longer term.

Expand Your Area of Responsibility

The third approach to creating indispensability to a corporation requires that you expand your area of responsibility.

The greater the breadth of your responsibility, the greater the value you provide to the organization. Professionals who can demonstrate the ability to wear many hats for a corporation will typically receive far more recognition and will be retained in periods of corporate downsizing. The other potential benefit to demonstrating a broader range of expertise is that corporations work very hard to reward the contributing professional in exceptional ways, which often include discretionary bonuses and increased levels of stock grants.

During my tenure as HR director for an aggressively growth-oriented organization, the staff levels at the company almost tripled over a three-year period. As the division grew, however, issues of office operations, customer service, and facilities concerns continued to surface. With no one being specifically responsible for those areas, I quickly offered to handle them myself. Within a short period, those functions reported directly under my "umbrella." Not only did my job become far more challenging and rewarding, the expanded role contributed to my upward mobility in the organization.

An additional benefit to acquiring broader-based experiences is that it helps keep you from becoming a "one-trick pony." The information technology executives I interviewed particularly reinforced this perspective. As several of them commented, the IT professional who focuses solely on a single technology, rather than developing a breadth of knowledge in a variety of technologies, runs the risk of losing his or her value to an organization. As one executive explained, "E-business is a good example. When it was first introduced it was the 'big thing' to many businesses but, over time, it became unimportant to the corporation."

While many individuals may be apprehensive about taking on unfamiliar areas, the executives I interviewed advised trusting one's skills and proven track record. A professional should operate under the assumption that he can figure anything out and function in any capacity. As one executive conveyed, "There is no limit to what the brain can process." In looking back over their careers, virtually every executive reinforced that in situations when they were given responsibility for areas outside of their own comfort and expertise, the expanded role proved to be far more challenging than they had originally expected.

One executive shared an experience in which he actually sought out a new area that provided greater opportunity to impact the bottom-line results for the company. Although this executive was an attorney by profession, by taking the initiative, he successfully acquired direct responsibility for the real estate function valued at almost $900 million—an assignment that had enormous visibility in his organization.

Another leader recalled a situation in his career when he actually created a new venture for the corporation. The executive observed that the company had several individual businesses that possessed similar operational and management issues. He proposed the creation of a separate enterprise that fully integrated the critical businesses under one umbrella. Not only did the corporate leaders accept the proposal, they appointed this individual to lead the division.

Beyond seeking out new areas of the business, the process of job expansion can often apply to one's existing function. Take the example of one executive who was responsible for the investor relations function. Over the course of six years, her role shifted from a traditional scope through a multitude of business changes: initial public offerings, acquisitions, and divestitures. The ability to expand her competence through the changing demands of the business helped broaden her expertise and increased her credibility and value to the corporation.

EXECUTIVE SUMMARY

If you want to attain a senior-level job in corporate America, you must develop an intellectual reservoir that is of great value to your organization.

At a time when all too many working professionals are concerned with issues of job security, the notion of developing one's indispensability may seem downright impossible. While it is true that no individual is guaranteed lifetime employment, the truth of the matter is that corporate leaders are concerned about their ability to attract and retain the ranks of top-performing individuals—particularly as the job market starts to shift dramatically with the retirement of baby boomer executives in the next five to ten years. Performing your job at an acceptable level may provide you with a paycheck, but it does nothing to create a perception of your value in the mind of your boss, nor does it ensure career advancement in a corporation. It is only the professional who can effectively demonstrate exceptional performance and establish herself as an expert in a specific area who will gain the attention of these influential leaders. This demonstrated expertise, however, is only the first step to being recognized by a corporation as one of its most valued employees.

Beyond establishing a proven track record of competency in your area of expertise, you must build a reputation of increased value to an organization, an objective that requires you to apply that same competency to other areas of the business. This job expansion and enrichment can occur within your functional area or extend across disciplines. As the executives reinforced, there is a direct correlation between your expertise to the critical drivers of the business and the level of value and recognition bestowed upon you by a corporation and its leaders. ◉

13 | WOMEN AT WORK: HAVE YOU REALLY COME A LONG WAY, BABY?

Although women have made progress in the workplace, they still remain far less successful in attaining senior-level positions than their male counterparts. Only eight *Fortune* 500 companies have a female CEO. In fact, in a random survey of 100 *Fortune* 500 corporations, women held only 21 percent of the senior-level positions. Perhaps even more disconcerting is that very few of those positions had direct bottom-line fiscal impact or influenced the profitability of the corporation.

As a result, more and more women are "jumping off" the corporate ladder as they see far fewer opportunities at too high a sacrifice. According to the U.S. Department of Labor, women are starting new ventures at a rate of 2:1 compared to men. For many women, becoming their own boss or starting an entrepreneurial venture may be a viable way to break through the glass ceiling; however, those women who still maintain the goal of success in large corporations are left to ask, "What's a girl to do?"

Rather than concede that male-dominated corporate cultures are the sole culprit of career barriers for women, my goal in interviewing this successful group of executives was to ask a different question. To what extent are these corporate barriers a result of women sabotaging themselves? Admittedly, it took some prodding for executives to speak candidly about the issue, but the feedback I received was quite enlightening. Indeed, the majority of executives believe, without question, that cultural barriers for women still exist in corporations. As one male executive commented, "The truth is that women have a more arduous road to success." In commenting on the good ol' boy networks that still exist in the corporate world, one female executive had this to say: "It's hard . . . women get tired of being so alone and often they are the only female in a male-dominated environment

Sometimes you just don't want to play golf or talk about sports just to fit in . . . Even after a number of years, respect and admiration for your accomplishments aside, you're still trying to fit in."

That being said, however, many of the executives admitted that in certain situations, a woman's behavior and actions contribute to a limited career progression. Based upon the executive's input, along with my own observations in the workplace, I have identified the five biggest mistakes women make in the corporate world. In addition, I will discuss the ways in which those missteps can be overcome.

Mistake #1—Focusing on Form over Substance

One common opinion shared by executives was that too many women focus on form rather than substance. In other words, they are too preoccupied with their appearance as professionals and not focused enough on the "substance" of their true business development. The following anecdotal example provided by a female executive perhaps best describes this behavior.

During a professional "mixer," the executive was discussing the challenges for women in the working world with a businesswoman she had just met. The woman began to describe the valuable guidance and coaching she received during her participation in a woman's "affinity" (support) group. When the executive asked about specific examples, she responded that she learned not to wear bracelets because they "jingle" and that she would not be taken seriously.

Many of the executives believed that women continue to place too much importance on cultivating the right look rather than on mastering key competencies. Interestingly enough, during one interview I was taken aback by the comment of a female executive who attributed her professional success, in part at least, to her attractiveness. As she put it, "I'm reasonably good to look at and that can be disarming to a lot of people." While it is true that appearance is important, and that being smart and attractive is a wonderful combination, looks alone will get you nowhere in the corporate world.

The "Marilyn Monroe" Profile

When in comes to embracing form over substance, many women gravitate to one end of the spectrum, which I call the Marilyn Monroe profile. Such women focus on their sex appeal, and take the approach of playing helpless in an attempt to allure men to their rescue. One executive shared the perfect example of this profile: "I worked with a woman who just couldn't give up the baby talk." Another executive relayed his frustration when he observed female colleagues applying lipstick while participating in business meetings.

While there is absolutely nothing wrong with being attractive, the women who hold the most powerful jobs in America have achieved that status with something other than their looks. Further, while portraying yourself as the damsel in distress may indeed attract a man's attention, and may even prove successful in the early stages of a job, such behavior will never earn you respect or propel your career in a significant way. Moreover, it is almost guaranteed to alienate female peers and subordinates whose support you will need at some point down the road.

Walk Like a Man, Talk Like a Man

At the other end of the form-over-substance spectrum is the woman who tries to emulate behaviors she observes in male colleagues or executives. In the 1980s, women were advised to dress the way a man would dress if he held her position. That advice translated into nearly a decade of masculine-styled women's power suits with stiff bow ties and austere styling.

Thankfully, business has become much more accepting of feminine clothing, and professional women have softened their appearance. However, many professional women, out of a misguided desire to be taken seriously, are still too preoccupied with acting like a man or trying to be one of the boys.

While there are many women who genuinely possess the same aggressive behaviors as their male counterparts, many of the executives interviewed felt that some women contrive certain behaviors that they deem necessary to getting ahead in the corporate world. For example, one senior executive relayed to me the instance of a female employee who "swore like a sailor," and it put him off because it seemed forced. "When I spoke to her about it, she said she thought it was expected. I told her, 'I could care less . . . I care about your work, that's it.'" He went on to say, "What she didn't realize was that the male executives became more preoccupied with her cursing than her ideas."

In many cases, a female professional will also have to overcome the preconceived ideas or programmed behaviors of male colleagues and senior management. For example, while attending one of my first executive staff meetings with the CEO, where I was the only woman present, I remember him using an expletive and then immediately turning to me and apologizing. At that very moment, realizing that he obviously thought I was offended by his remark, I knew that my response would dictate how I was perceived in the future. I needed to respond in a way that conveyed that I was no different than any other staff member, without insulting his gentlemanly approach. I took the humorous tact of covering my ears and responding, "Oh, my virgin ears!" Everyone had a good laugh over it. More importantly, he continued to swear in my presence and never apologized to me for it again.

The fact of the matter is that in dealing with a variety of human beings, female professionals will encounter some men who have preconceived notions and engrained behaviors about women at work. Their motivations are not always devious, nor is their conduct intended to be dismissive or offensive toward females. Sometimes the behavior is simply a product of their upbringing. As one executive confessed, "I'm from the old school, and I came from a family that hugged each other . . . at work, I've had to learn to be very careful because in today's work environment that's considered inappropriate."

Some executives were even more candid in affirming that situations of sexual advances and inappropriate comments toward women still exist in the working world. As one female executive advises, "The toughest thing for a women is to completely maintain a 'poker face' when confronted by inappropriate behavior and sexual advances from colleagues, middle management, or even vendors . . . If you can handle yourself with the precision of a surgeon, you gain a lot of respect."

While such advice may sound like "grin and bear it," the executives interviewed stressed that they are not advocating that women tolerate inappropriate behavior for the sake of their careers. What they did caution, however, was that women must choose their battles very carefully. If every situation involving undesirable conduct results in a mushroom cloud of reproach and accusations being detonated by the female professional, the woman is likely to find herself being treated as Typhoid Mary throughout the organization. As one female executive commented, "If I took issue with every inappropriate or condescending remark, that's what I'd be known for . . . being the overly sensitive one."

The objective for the female professional, or any professional for that matter, is to develop an effective balance between form and substance. If a woman is to err on one of those sides, however, she is always better served by substance than style. I draw the analogy to building a house. You may design the most beautiful and intricate home, but if it rests on a weak foundation, it is inevitably destined for collapse. The female professional must first establish the foundation of business credibility through peak performance. Once that is obtained, her natural style, or form, becomes an enhancement to the overall professional package.

Mistake #2—Not Making Use of Effective Feminine Qualities

While the approach to developing a strong business expertise is no different for men than it is for women, the executives interviewed asserted that women do possess certain innate behaviors that may actually prove to be influential to their career success.

The executives stressed that they were referring to substantive behaviors rather than demeaning approaches such as flirtation or acquiescence. As one executive expressed, "Women tend to be far more nurturing than men, and it can give them an advantage . . . they need to embrace their differences." However, the more difficult part for the female executive is seizing opportunities in which to openly and comfortably demonstrate those behaviors, without the behavior looking forced.

Humor, for example, was one behavior that a number of female executives cited as being highly effective. One executive vice president expressed that she uses humor to defuse emotionally charged situations. Another executive stated that using a witty, well-placed retort with a difficult colleague, rather than creating a heated argument, minimizes the risk of being labeled "a bitch on wheels."

I also discussed with these executives the possibilities for employing compassion as a substantive behavior in the workplace. For example, how many times have you interacted with a male colleague who appeared stressed or frustrated? Yet in how many of those instances did you actually ask for the specifics of the situation or probe further? And when you did ask, did you think about how the answer could actually help you and your career?

Specifically, compassion accomplishes the following:

- It establishes you as a sounding board and confidante.
- It allows you to gain insight into that individual.

In the case of a boss or superior who needs to lighten his or her workload, a show of compassion may also result in your receiving a special project, which will serve your career as much as it helps them.

Mistake #3—Making It Personal

A large number of executives commented that in their observations of heated debates or confrontations, women often have the tendency to "take it personally." As one executive described, "You can see guys in a meeting disagreeing with each other, even getting angry, and then the meeting is over and they're laughing and talking about the game they saw the night before. Too often, women leave the same meeting and they are furious. Worse still, is that women will often harbor that anger for several days."

The lesson here is that sometimes business decisions result in professionals sharing strong opinions in a very forceful manner. Female professionals must understand that in most cases, the aggressive behaviors demonstrated in the workplace revolve around business issues rather than being personal attacks. As one executive put it, "A corporation is a business unit, not a family. If a woman is too focused on being liked and getting along with everyone, she can lose sight altogether of the business objective."

In hearing the comments of many of the executives, particularly the men, what was made clear was that women must learn to approach difficult business situations in a more objective fashion. Women who demonstrate a resentful approach to confrontation or disagreement simply perpetuate a stereotype that women are too "emotional" or "sensitive" in their roles as professionals or managers.

Mistake #4—Hanging Back

First off, I must give credit for the term "hanging back" to one of the executives, who used it in his observation that women are too often reluctant to volunteer for an assignment or project. In my own experience as a senior executive, I too have noticed the same thing. I have always found it surprising that for all the concern professional women express about the biases, diminished opportunity, and even discrimination in the workplace, few of them seize the opportunity to gain recognition. While it is a fact that inequalities between men and women do exist in the workplace, particularly around the issue of compensation, it is the opinion of many executives that women seem to acquiesce to this role by not positioning themselves aggressively enough.

The point here is that women must take responsibility for driving their success, and the quickest way to make headway is by capitalizing on any opportunity that presents itself. The understanding that women are a minority in the corporate world dictates that women must be more aggressive in creating a platform on which to perform. Fair or unfair doesn't matter; do the math. If for every project or promotion, there is one woman competing for every five men, the women is going to have to be that much better. If you don't get in the game, you can't outperform your competition.

It is not enough to simply take on a project when presented with the opportunity. Still, according to the executives interviewed, that is what many women do. Women need to actively seek out and solicit projects and assignments. While some may argue that such an approach is contrived or political, the executives interviewed disagreed; creating opportunity and lightening the load for your boss *is* your responsibility as a professional. Whether you are a secretary or senior sales representative, taking initiative to further demonstrate your performance is necessary if you are to set yourself apart from the male crowd. As one executive remarked, "Men are far more willing to volunteer for an assignment than women. In my experience, women miss out on opportunities because they don't want to appear pushy."

My advice is to start slowly with this tactic. When you find yourself in conversation with your boss on another work-related matter, simply take a minute to ask if there is anything he or she might need done. Leave it that open-ended and vague. Don't worry; most managers will seize any opening to delegate an assignment, as long as they believe you are competent enough to handle the project. Now if they say "No," do not take the escape route and tell yourself, "Okay, I asked and he didn't give me an assignment, so that's it!" Remember, that was only one experience. Follow-up is everything. Once your boss observes a consistent pattern of your willingness to take on additional work, he or she will start coming to you . . . guaranteed!

If true success is your goal, then you need to stand up and compete. This means demonstrating your willingness to initiate additional work and volunteering for special assignments that arise. Otherwise, "hanging back" ultimately means "hanging it up."

Mistake #5—Working the Concession Stand

When it comes to family demands, women have a reputation for requesting more corporate concessions than their male counterparts. As one male executive so succinctly put it, "When it comes to family duties, most men have a choice, but most women do not." While that may sound chauvinistic to some, the harsh reality is that there is a tremendous amount of truth to that statement. Right or wrong, the majority of familial demands and obligations still tend to fall on the shoulders of the woman.

In further discussing this issue with executives, the majority of them agreed that for women to attain higher-level positions, they must make the concessions (or sacrifices) themselves rather than asking the corporation to accommodate Susie's doctor appointment or Johnny's baseball game. As one executive put it, "Women have the same opportunity to make sacrifices as men do."

Interestingly enough, the family obligations of the female executives I interviewed typically fell into three categories:

- Single or divorced with no children, or with grown children
- Married with children, with a stay-at-home husband
- Married with children, with full-time nanny

These alternative support situations are identified here to highlight the harsh realities of sacrifice and compromise that a woman must consider before pursuing an executive career.

As one executive expressed, "A woman cannot be the care-giver and a senior executive. There has to be a support system in place to equalize the demands for the female professional . . . otherwise, forget it."

While it is true that many corporate cultures are far more sensitive to the plight of the working mother, it does not mean that there isn't a price that accompanies that understanding. The truth of the matter is that in the corporate world, there are no brownie points for being a working mother. It is important that women remember that balancing family and work demands is about personal choice; the female professional who wants true corporate success must deliver the results without seeking special allowances. Once she begins asking for time off, or a modified work schedule, no matter how strong her performance, her career advancement potential is often over before it starts.

The good news, however, is that some executives do see an improved flexibility on the part of some business leaders toward family demands. One female executive shared this example: "When I had my son I was traveling seven days a week, dragging my baby and the nanny with me everywhere. After a year of that schedule, I knew I had to make a choice. I told my boss that I was going to resign to take care of my son. Though a father of six children himself, my boss became very angry. Shortly thereafter, though, he proposed modifications to my job and travel schedule which allowed me to continue with the company."

Many corporations are attempting to raise their management team's awareness and sensitivity to their employees' family obligations. In fact, many corporate cultures are instituting support groups and developing programs that address the needs of female professionals. On a global level, many organizations have realized it is imperative that they address these real-life concerns in order to recruit and retain staff and promote healthy morale. However, for the female professional who wants to be the next executive vice president or chief operating officer, spending extensive amounts of time championing these issues won't get you to the top . . . it just won't. In the numerous good ol' boy networks that still exist today, you'll be labeled an activist, and that is not one of the critical competencies sought by senior executives.

EXECUTIVE SUMMARY

While many working women have successfully broken through the glass ceiling that exists in many organizations by achieving high-powered, high-paying corporate positions, the truth is that women still have to go a long way toward achieving parity with male executives. As one executive put it, "Right now the corporate world is a product of a male bastion, so women need to figure out how to work on those terms."

While all professionals face the challenge of developing the right skills and demonstrating their effectiveness as a team player, women need to work twice as hard to establish professional credibility in an organization. Rightly or wrongly, the corporate arena is highly competitive, and there are far more men vying for the top jobs than women.

If women are to continue to make progress in their climb up the corporate ladder, their focus must remain on developing substantive performance while capitalizing on innate female behaviors. The key is for women to recognize and embrace their differences rather than adapting behaviors they deem as highly valued or expected by a corporation and its leaders. ◉

14 | DESPERATELY SEEKING SALARY

In light of many recent corporate scandals, much press has been given to the exorbitant, and sometimes undeserved, level of compensation that many senior-level executives receive. As I learned in my many years as a senior level human resources executive and in talks about the issue of salary with working professionals at all levels, most people believe that senior executives are primarily motivated by money. This perspective reminds me of a time several years ago. The CEO I worked with, in making final hiring decisions, would ask the candidates to rank the following motivators in order of personal importance:

- ◆ Challenge
- ◆ Money
- ◆ Work environment

If the candidate placed "work environment" at the top of the list, he or she would not be hired. It was the executive's opinion that an executive who paid more attention to internal environment, rather than challenge or financial rewards, was neither results oriented nor achievement driven. This top executive was interested in hiring professionals who were motivated to impact the financial performance of the corporation. At first I found his interview approach and his logic to be ridiculous. Over time, however, I began to see a distinct pattern in the quality of employee performance by those individuals who found money and challenge to be the greater motivating factors for their career decisions. In fact, in the rare instances when an individual was still hired even after selecting work environment as their primary motivation, the person typically failed in the job.

Interestingly enough, in discussing the issue of compensation as a motivator to the executives interviewed, most commented that while money was important to each of them, they tended to be driven by the challenge provided by their work far more than the money it provided. As one executive cited, "I've always been motivated by interesting and challenging work. Money has never been that big of a deal for me. I guess I always believed that if I achieved my objectives then the money would follow."

This "field of dreams" mentality was indeed prevalent with the majority of the executives, though there were a few exceptions. One executive, for example, openly admitted that he is far more motivated by money than by challenge. "It doesn't matter what I do . . . even if it is a boring job, if it pays well, I'm there." He went on to say, "If another company called me tomorrow and would pay me more money, I'd leave this company in a second."

The Greater the Performance, the Greater the Money

As the majority of executives expressed, the truth about the working world is that increased performance and responsibility lead to increased rewards. Essentially, the message from most executives is simple: "When you deliver the results, the money will follow."

The other significant point made by many of the executives is that true wealth comes from receiving equity in a company through stock options and restricted stock grants. As one executive commented, "You don't get rich from annual increases." These financial incentives are reserved for top-performing employees and are directly linked to those positions that significantly influence the success of the corporation.

If an individual is to achieve such rewards, he or she must demonstrate exceptional performance and strive to impact the fiscal performance of a corporation in a significant way. In the words of one executive, "The outcome for delivering value to a company is that you don't need to ever have your hat in hand."

Security Versus Luxury

Contrary to the opinions of many working professionals, who believe that executives spend most of their money on extravagant luxuries and a lavish lifestyle, I found the executives to be quite conservative in this respect. While most of them make a significant amount of money, their lifestyle, as they described it, tended to be fairly modest. Certainly, they possess nice homes and cars, but they talked more about the issue of money in terms of personal convenience and stability rather than a source of power or an ego symbol. Remembering that the majority of these individuals grew up in modest households, it stands to reason that many view compensation as a means of providing for their families and building a nest egg of security for themselves.

One interesting observation made by several of the executives is that in building financial security, they are able to serve as better executives for the corporation. When they commented about the greedy behavior observed in the corporate world, they described individuals who made decisions based on protecting personal wealth rather than the well-being of the company itself. For example, some executives observed that colleagues who were nearing retirement often demonstrated a propensity to advocate conservative business strategies, even when taking a more risky approach could result in greater longer-term financial gain for the corporation. In speaking about his own actions, one executive shared the following: "Sometimes with executives the more money and stock they have, the more inclined they are to protect it. In my case, being financially secure is liberating—I do the right thing for the corporation because I don't have to worry about feeding my family."

That being said, however, these same individuals also shared that as executives, they do pay attention to their compensation as compared to what their colleagues are paid. At the senior levels, it isn't so much the actual amount of money they are being paid. Rather, these individuals view compensation as a measuring stick of their value as it is perceived by the CEO and the company's board members. As one executive put it, "Compensation at this level is more about it being a function of knowing that I'm highly thought of by my boss." Another executive articulated it this way, "I'm concerned about being fairly compensated relative to my peers. I don't have to be the highest paid executive. I realize that compensation is not an absolute, it's relative." Contrary to what many working professionals might think, employees at all levels, including the most senior executives, pay attention (and are often preoccupied) to the amount of money their peers are being paid.

The Balancing Act

As it relates to managing the compensation of their staff members, many of the executives I interviewed bemoaned the fact that compensation is the single most challenging and emotionally charged issue in the corporate world. Managers continually struggle with how to reward and retain top performers while operating within budgetary constraints. While the issue of compensation remains an ongoing battle between a corporation and its employees, most corporate cultures strive to reward its top performers above and beyond traditional salary increases.

As a number of these top executives shared, this "pay for performance" philosophy is a significant departure from the way in which old school cultures rewarded performance.

One female executive shared an example about receiving her first merit increase back in the 1970s. Her boss told her that while she was indeed the top performer in the department, he was going to allocate the larger increase to her male counterpart. He explained that the male employee's wife did not work, while she had a husband who was employed. As this executive commented, "I remember thinking that his decision was wrong, but I never would have said anything to him about it."

Unlike many professionals of previous generations, professionals today are far more informed and savvy about market trends and industry averages relative to pay structures and salary ranges. People are far more likely to question and even challenge their pay packages around a whole host of issues. The question then becomes, "Is taking issue with one's compensation a career-limiting maneuver?" In asking executives, I found there to be two distinct schools of thought on the matter.

For at least half of the group, the belief was that challenging the compensation package is detrimental to the success of the individual. As one executive simply put it, "It's just a bad idea!" They believe the attitude creates a negative perception among senior managers about the employee. Such behavior is interpreted to be indicative of the professional being more focused on money than on performance and contribution. The other half of the group, however, views the behavior as acceptable and, in some cases, even welcomed by the executive and management team.

These senior professionals clarified that it does come down to one's approach in addressing compensation concerns. As many of the executives explained, there are definite salary-seeking approaches that are negatively received by corporations and their leaders.

The Double Standard

While a number of the executives openly shared how they pay attention to their own compensation relative to their peers, when it comes to their own subordinates addressing perceived inequities, many of these executives are far less tolerant of the behavior. In their minds, the difference is that with staff members the issue isn't about perceived value, it's about the money. To quote a term from a former boss, this undesired behavior is best labeled as the "Theory of Compensation Relativity." Simply put, the employee is content with his pay until he learns that someone else is making more money in a comparable position. Suddenly, the content employee becomes highly dissatisfied with his pay. While companies attempt to manage the problem by emphasizing to employees the importance of keeping salaries confidential, it never works. Colleagues eventually do talk to each other about compensation.

Many of the opinions shared by executives actually contradict their own actions. For instance, after learning of senior colleagues' compensation as compared to their own, a handful of the executives interviewed actually spoke to their CEOs about the disparity. It should come as no surprise to know that these executives tended to be far more accepting of junior staffers challenging their compensation package.

The majority of the executives, however, view this approach to be career suicide. Being pegged as the compensation complainer is a difficult branding to overcome. What professionals must understand is that two people can easily perform in a comparable, or even the exact same, job without any requirement that each be paid the same amount of money. Most employees fail to consider that various factors influence compensation: length of service, previous work history, promotional opportunities, and individual performance. The other problem with this approach is that it often becomes a very personal issue for the manager or executive. As one senior person put it, "I get pissed off because the person assumes that I don't know how to take care of my employees!"

Along similar lines is the issue of salary grades and ranges. In my discussions with the executives, there tended to be far more flexibility and willingness to discuss concerns and challenges relating to salary structures than specific pay issues. The reason for this was that in most corporations, it is difficult to effectively communicate the methodology behind pay grades and structures to all levels of employees. Frequently the complexities built into such programs—quartiles, minimums, midpoints, and maximums—create an inherent distrust among many employees and result in constant questions and challenges about equitable compensation. I believe that these issues are far more tolerable to most senior executives because the nature of challenges are far more process-driven and depersonalized. The professional's issue is less "mine versus his" and more focused on understanding the overall compensation system.

The Stick-Up

The other significant compensation "no-no" involves what a few executives termed as the "stick-up." This behavior typically rears its ugly head when the demand for certain jobs far exceeds the supply of qualified talent. Numerous examples were shared about the legal, IT, nursing, and pharmacology fields, just to name a few. During extreme market shortages for talent, the professional will place monetary demands on the corporation or threaten to go elsewhere.

Executives caution professionals about this mindset because staffing and business conditions will eventually change over time. During situations of peak demand, the individual may indeed have their company "over a barrel." However, once the demand subsides or the supply begins to meet the demands for that expertise, the stick-up artist is in big trouble. As one executive crudely put it, "If you've established yourself as the corporate whore going to the highest bidder, that label will stick with you throughout your career and can ultimately ruin you in the long run."

Full Disclosure

One other interesting dynamic that relates to executive compensation revolves around the public disclosure of salary. A number of the executives interviewed for this book are among the five highest paid individuals in their organizations, and the company is required to report that compensation data in their annual financial disclosures.

It may surprise many working professionals to know that this public disclosure is often a sore spot for the impacted executives. As one executive remarked, "I'd prefer to be a private person." Several of these folks commented on the offhanded remarks and awkward situations involving their salaries that arise from friends, neighbors, acquaintances, and even family members. One executive shared a time when a distant relative remarked to his mother about the money he was making; another executive shared that a few members of the congregation made flippant remarks about his pay as he was leaving the Sunday church service. Such comments are disconcerting to most of these successful individuals. As one executive shared, "I know it comes with the territory, but it still makes me very uncomfortable." While many of these executives enjoy the challenge and rewards that accompany holding the most influential positions, when it comes to the world knowing exactly what they are being paid, the amount of their annual bonus, or the value of their equity share, most of them would just as soon keep it to themselves.

EXECUTIVE SUMMARY

Everyone wants to make more money, and few professionals believe that they are being adequately compensated for their efforts. While it is natural and normal to want to make more money, professionals need to understand that no short-cuts exist to achieving greater compensation in the corporate world. The key is to expend more energy on refining your skills and developing competency and less time worrying about what everyone else is earning. At the corporate level, compensation plans can be very complex and difficult for a professional to fully comprehend. In cases where you do not understand your company's pay programs or philosophies, it is completely acceptable to discuss these issues with your boss. As the executives reinforced, though, it is when you begin to personalize the compensation issues that you can find yourself maneuvering through a minefield. ◉

15 | TAKING CRITICISM LIKE A CHAMP

Regardless of whether you hold a senior-level position, the work is demanding in most of today's corporations. The number of hours worked by most U.S. employees in the average workweek has steadily crept up over the past two decades. Today the average employee logs approximately forty-nine hours per week, not including commuting. Coupled with the demands of a family and a personal life, most employees feel as though they are running to catch up. They are caught in a constant cycle of trying to make both ends meet in the middle—and coming up short. Considering how much energy people expend in simply maintaining their careers, let alone moving them forward, is it any wonder that most professionals are defensive about criticism related to their performance?

It's a fundamental law of human nature. No one enjoys hearing criticism about his or her work. Over the course of your career, you may learn to effectively *listen* to critical input, but that doesn't mean that you *welcome* such feedback. Interestingly enough, the executives interviewed did suggest that their top performers not only sought out constructive criticism but are actually far tougher on themselves than any boss ever could be.

By their own admission, however, these senior executives—top performers in their own right—have also struggled with accepting negative feedback and demonstrated negative responses similar to many other professionals. However, each has learned over the course of his or her career to welcome the feedback as a means of improving performance and developing effective skills and competencies on the job. As we discussed the typical responses encountered when giving constructive criticism, the executives shared four common behaviors.

The Filter

As one executive described this behavior, "It's the individual who hears what they want to hear versus what is actually being conveyed." This behavior is detrimental to a professional's success. If you cannot absorb the full meaning of the feedback, there is little hope that you will make the necessary correction in your performance. If the behavior continues, it may lead to further disciplinary action and in the extreme, may result in termination.

The Shut Down

With this behavior, the professional locks in on the first negative comment regarding his or her performance and ceases to hear any explanation or examples of the problem. Executives explain that often they can visibly observe the individual becoming paralyzed over the critique.

This behavior is problematic in a healthy exchange between the manager and employee. More often than not, the discussion typically becomes a one-way conversation. The manager, seeing the employee "locked up" on a piece of criticism, will often attempt to alleviate the tension by continuously talking through the issue. If the employee cannot find a way to re-engage back into the conversation, there will be no healthy exchange of information. The entire performance appraisal process then becomes academic. The employee leaves the session having only heard the negative comments and potentially losing all credibility with the manager.

On the other hand, if the employee can manage to regroup after having thoroughly processed both the positive and negative comments, he or she can request a subsequent meeting with the manager to discuss certain points about the review. If done openly, such a meeting can result in a productive discussion for both the manager and the employee and resolve any outstanding performance issues.

The Fighter

When receiving constructive criticism, the fighter quickly becomes argumentative about the negative feedback. According to a large number of the executives interviewed, this behavior tends to be emotionally charged and defensive. The professional who demonstrates this attacking behavior is more consumed with contradicting the feedback than listening to and absorbing the information being imparted by the manager.

The difficulty with this combative approach to performance feedback is that it not only hinders any opportunity for an open exchange between boss and subordinate, it creates such discomfort for the manager that he or she will cease any further explanation or clarification about the performance feedback. In the extreme, this behavior will result in a significant strain on the relationship. It may even result in the manager's ceasing to provide the employee with any further developmental coaching—and an employee that can't be coached is more often than not eventually shown the door.

The Flight

This all-too-common behavior is easy to recognize—once a criticism is shared by the manager, the professional high-tails it out of the meeting as soon as possible. There is virtually no exchange between manager and employee with this approach. Unlike the fighter, this individual will nod in an understanding fashion, but internally he is planning his exit strategy. Many executives commented that early on in their careers, they too demonstrated this behavior. However, as they matured into their positions and their career, they learned to accept constructive criticism in a more open way. As one executive shared, "I got nicked up in a performance appraisal for being too arrogant. Rather than hearing my boss out, I just got mad . . . and I stayed mad for about six months. After finally coming out of my funk, I have always taken a more accepting approach to feedback."

This flight behavior is detrimental as it also leads to one-way communication. Unless the individual can later regroup his thoughts and openly discuss the appraisal, nothing constructive will result from the process.

Perception Is Reality

Regardless of what any professional may think about the specific performance feedback, or the individual providing the critique, the fact remains that the perceptions of others regarding one's performance do impact one's potential success in the corporate world. Even in situations where the manager is ineffective at providing constructive feedback, the employee has a vested interest in obtaining clarity on the areas for improvement and development. As one executive put it, "You better try on every idea even if you think your boss has his head up his ass. You need to view the feedback as being generous to your success rather than a personal attack." While the message may be harsh, it is indeed true.

The reality is that some managers are ill equipped to effectively write and clearly convey performance feedback. That said, a professional must still be an active participant in the performance appraisal process. Otherwise, the person runs the risk of never obtaining a clear understanding of what to do differently in one's job. While being solely responsible for one's career might seem unfair or burdensome, it is the reality of managing success in the corporate world. If there is to be an effective exchange between you and your manager, you must take a positive, proactive approach to the process. Here are some critical strategies you can use to facilitate a healthy performance discussion.

Seek Feedback Throughout the Year

Rather than waiting for his or her annual performance appraisal, the smart professional aims to get continuous performance feedback. Get out of the mindset that constructive criticism is a once-a-year occurrence. Operating under the assumption that "no news is good news" is a potential career landmine. Too many working professionals opt to wait for the performance "autopsy" rather than collecting input and diagnosing areas for improvement throughout the year. Managers are busy people, and if you assume that your superior will tell you if there is a problem, you are playing too passive a role in managing your success. Again, some managers are better at providing consistent performance feedback, but assuming that someone else will manage the process is a potential mistake that could cost you your career.

One executive shared a past experience with a boss who solicited the employee's opinion about his performance after an important meeting. While the executive was taken aback by his boss's open approach, he understood the intent of his inquiry. As he explained, "You never stop learning—even when you're the boss yourself; he wanted me to pay attention to what he was doing and how he was doing it, and he wanted me to think about how to continuously improve my performance."

Employees too must seize opportunities, particularly after doing a task for the first time, to solicit feedback about their performance. Over the course of a career, one can obtain critical feedback from all levels of the organization, including peers and subordinates. While many employees believe that this approach somehow demonstrates weakness or a lack of self-confidence, most of the executives disagree. As the executives reinforced, it is the self-assured professional who openly seeks out constructive feedback about his or her performance.

Keep Track of Wins and Losses

Managers are often taught to manage employee performance through a method known as "critical incidents." This process tracks significant achievements and errors by documenting those specific instances throughout the year that should be addressed in the appraisal process. Just as the approach can be highly effective for managers, it can also be useful to professionals as well. By keeping score of your activities throughout the year, you can track your individual wins and losses and be better prepared for a performance discussion.

While the appraisal process can be complicated and daunting to everyone concerned, the fact remains that it is often the only formalized process for setting the record straight on your performance. The use of critical incidents can assist you in several ways:

- ◆ It assists you in developing self-assessment skills.
- ◆ It results in a well-rounded assessment of performance.
- ◆ It creates opportunities to provide concrete examples that illustrate positive performance.

◆ It helps you develop a more open mindset toward both positive and negative feedback.

Your ability to provide a comprehensive and objective self-assessment of your performance will illustrate professional maturity and an ingrained desire to succeed.

Listen, Listen, Listen

It is one thing to know the performance factors that lead to achievement, but without the ability to truly hear critical feedback, you will never identify the variance between your actual performance and the desired standards. Active listening requires you to openly approach any discussion assuming that there will be more negative comments than positive ones. This assumption will keep you from reverting to defensive behaviors that prove counterproductive to the discussion. If you approach any feedback as welcomed coaching, it is more likely that you will actively process the critique.

Effective "active" listening does require physical action. One of the first steps of active listening occurs while the feedback is being shared. Positive gestures such as nodding of the head and taking notes conveys that you are truly absorbing the information in a thoughtful way. The point here is that these behaviors need to become a natural part of your demeanor rather than a role that you play during the review process. "Faking it," will only lead to failure or, at best, mediocre performance.

The other significant approach to active listening is through the use of clarifying statements or questions, such as "So what you're saying is," or "If I understand your coaching what you're telling me to do differently is. . . ." This approach immediately establishes an environment of trust between the manager and employee. It acknowledges your understanding of the feedback, even if you disagree with the assessment. Equally important, exhibiting receptive behavior sets a positive tone and makes for a far more productive interaction on points of disagreement between the manager and employee.

Don't Confuse Effort with Results

A common trap that many professionals fall into is in confusing effort and hours worked with achieved results. One executive gave the example of coaching a subordinate on her substandard results. The employee's immediate comeback was, "But I've been working so hard." The executive had to stop and tell the employee that while the long hours and the effort was indeed appreciated, the lack of results was disconcerting and unacceptable to the executive. As the executive clarified for the employee, "It's not a will issue, it's a skill issue."

In my own professional experience, I have found that when people work an excessive amount of hours on a continual basis, it is easy for them to assume that their effort somehow overshadows any shortcomings in performance. Unfortunately, with most managers, that assessment is simply not the case. Success requires both effort and delivery of results. To achieve success in a corporation, or anywhere else for that matter, you must listen to feedback on all aspects of your performance rather than only those elements you deem as important.

Don't Kick It Upstairs!

While it can be tough to endure criticism, don't ever go over your boss's head to complain about your performance appraisal. You'll be stepping into a veritable corporate minefield. As one executive articulated, "Do employees really think that I'm going to overrule their boss? Are they really that stupid?" The truth is that if you want to quickly alienate yourself and orchestrate an adversarial relationship with your supervisor, publicly challenge their management skills with their boss.

Open communication within a chain of command is often recommended in employee handbooks as a means of resolving conflict, but let me set the record straight—it is a bad idea. Yet all too many professionals make this mistake. What people fail to recognize is that with most appraisal processes, all levels within the hierarchy have not only read the performance appraisal, they have signed off on it as well. You must remember that the individuals who operate one or two levels above your immediate supervisor typically have far less exposure to your individual performance and therefore will rely on the credibility of your boss's assessment.

Involving your manager's boss in a performance matter is a very personal and emotional issue to most managers. Such an approach will only create a wedge between you and your boss. It will also label you as troublemaker with senior management. Further, this tactic may potentially destroy any opportunity for you to receive valuable coaching, let alone a future with the company.

EXECUTIVE SUMMARY

To effectively develop yourself as a professional, you must be able to critically assess your shortcomings and developmental needs—and respect the assessment of others concerning your deficiencies. As such assessment relates to performance appraisals and feedback sessions, you must be able to have healthy and open exchanges with your manager and peers. View feedback as a developmental tool rather than a personal criticism. The reality check is that if you can't face your own shortcomings, you will go nowhere in a corporation. Moreover, you will more than likely be labeled the corporate "victim," who blames everyone else for your stagnant career. ⊙

16 | PERFORMANCE IMPROVEMENT PLANS: IS IT TIME TO UPDATE YOUR RESUME?

Most professionals in today's corporate world adopt a "no news is good news" approach to performance feedback. Meanwhile, as their colleagues are given prestigious assignments and promoted, these employees continue to sit idly by, erroneously assuming that someone will let them know if their performance is lacking. Such employees operate under the ostrich approach, sticking their heads in the sand and not proactively seeking out constructive criticism. Meanwhile, their careers may be stagnating or even in jeopardy. By the time these employees wake up and address the issue, it's often too late—they are on the receiving end of a disciplinary action, or they've lost too much ground to smarter, savvier employees.

In theory, managers should initiate and provide consistent feedback on employee performance, particularly if issues are brewing. The difficulty for many supervisors in effectively managing performance, however, is that there is never enough time to do so. Most corporations require managers to oversee a function and to serve as an individual contributor. The reality check is that there are only so many hours in a day, and the heavy weight of dual responsibilities often infringes on the time that a manager can actually devote to the performance management process. As one executive commented, "The performance management process is an extremely important function that no one has time to do."

The other factor impacting performance management relates to a manager's skill in providing both positive and negative feedback to the professional. Most managers are simply not skillful at providing specific feedback in terms that most employees understand. As one executive shared, "I generally believe that performance weaknesses should be communicated at a much earlier stage, but I often find that managers are either reluctant to share them or very poor at explaining the problem."

As it relates to skill, all too often managers know the performance standards, but they have difficulty effectively communicating these expectations to the underperforming employee. Management's inability to clearly define the required improvements typically translates to vague explanations and poor coaching. In the absence of clear and direct performance expectations being provided to the employee, it is highly unlikely that the problem will be corrected. Further, if the employee is remiss in seeking out further clarification about deficiencies, he or she has absolutely no idea of the changes that need to be implemented to effectively meet performance expectations. The manager then leaves the discussion under the assumption that the message has been successfully conveyed and that all is well.

This poor communication typically results in the performance issue that escalates into a much more serious situation for the employee. Sooner or later—and usually sooner—the manager will solicit the involvement of the human resources department in preparing a corrective action for the employee regarding his substandard performance.

The paternalistic style of management that many corporations demonstrated in previous decades has created an entitlement mentality in many employees. Even a shockingly high percentage of younger professionals expect a corporation to manage their careers and hold their hands through any professional bumps in the road. If you are still harboring this mentality, get over it! It is not the sole responsibility of your manager to ensure that you are performing at an acceptable level. Every professional has the obligation to assume ownership for his or her demonstrated performance. If you don't devote your full attention to understanding any concerns management may have about your performance, and, more importantly, demonstrate the commitment to addressing them, you will be destined for failure.

What Does "Progressive Discipline" Really Mean?

Ask any executive about the length of time it takes to actually terminate a poorly performing employee, and you typically hear the response, "Too long!" The process of disciplining an employee is, as the title implies, a progressive one. Each step of the process is usually intended to reinforce the gravity of the situation to the employee.

In a perfect world, the disciplinary process is designed to correct substandard performance and get the employee back on track. In the real world, however, once a manager has talked to the employee about performance deficiencies, and those areas for improvement are not immediately corrected, the disciplinary process often becomes nothing more than a formality marking steps toward the employee's termination.

The inherent problem with the disciplinary process is that all too often corporations, and specifically the human resources department, make the process far more cumbersome than is actually necessary. The fear of litigation and charges of discrimination often drive an organization to mandate an inordinate amount of documentation pertaining to the employee's performance deficiencies. This approach of "building a case" is laborious and can take up to six months before the company is finally rid of the substandard employee.

Many corporate soldiers will defend this process, arguing that the progressive disciplinary process can serve as a successful tool for correcting poor performance. According to several of the executives interviewed, in some cases the severity of a performance improvement plan may jolt the employee into addressing the performance concerns. Most of the time, however, the process serves as one more piece of documentation toward the termination process. As one executive honestly shared, "My experience is that performance improvement plans are used far more often to simply get rid of the employee."

In talking with the executives about the issue of employee discipline and termination, I found that many of them tended to toe the party line, commenting on how their organizations truly focus on the success and development of their employees. My own observations and professional experience with many managers, however, contradict this ringing endorsement of the corporate world. While not every business leader approaches the process of employee development in a callous and cavalier manner, the simple truth is that the demanding nature of corporate America allows little time for extended coaching and often cultivates management's impatience and intolerance for substandard performance. As a result, managers often tend to give an individual only one chance to get it right, or at least show an encouraging level of performance improvement.

How Does Progressive Discipline Process Actually Work?

In theory, the structure of the progressive disciplinary process is designed to coach employees to improved performance over a reasonable and effective period of time. Within each step progression, more severe consequences are communicated to the substandard performer. The process typically

includes the following steps (which may vary in each individual company):

- Verbal warnings
- Written performance improvement plan
- Written progress reports
- Final written warning
- Termination

Verbal discussions are the first step in the process of correcting substandard performance. These "call outs" may be
shared as part of an annual performance appraisal or conducted as separate discussions. Typically, at this point in the
process, the objective of the exchange is to openly discuss the
areas for improvement and provide coaching on the actions
necessary to correct deficiencies.

If the expected performance changes are not successfully achieved, the disciplinary process then evolves into a
more formalized performance improvement plan. While the
label associated with the action appears supportive to the
employee, let's be clear—this mechanism is nothing but a formal corrective and disciplinary action. It should be further
understood that once the process has escalated to this level of
formal documentation, in most cases, the manager is quickly
losing faith in your ability to correct the problem and meet
acceptable performance standards.

As many of the executives reinforced, too often the
employee will expend energy on disputing the issues rather
than attempting to fully comprehend the problem. As one

executive put it, "Some people don't hear the message until they see it on paper as a performance improvement plan with a consequence attached to the failure to improve."

Regardless of whether an individual simply ignores the early warning signs of a disciplinary action, or is simply incapable of meeting the required performance standards, the outcome remains the same—the employee's days are numbered.

Now You've Got a Decision to Make

Once the documentation is drafted, the difficult reality of a performance improvement plan is that the grains of sand are quickly sifting through the corporate hourglass.

At this point you must decide whether to commit every ounce of energy to succeeding in your job or, to put it bluntly, getting the hell out of the organization.

If your decision is to attempt to correct your performance deficiencies, the first step is to meet with your manager to convey in no uncertain terms that you are committed to achieving success. This positive reinforcement may fall on deaf ears, but in many instances, it can influence your supervisor to be more willing to give you a second chance.

Beyond communicating the desire to succeed, the most positive action you can employ is to make absolutely certain that you understand exactly what needs to be done differently on the job and the specific results that must be achieved. If your manager struggles with providing this information, tell her that you remain unclear of expectations. Ask for them in writing, if you need to. Keep prodding until you obtain the answers. This is no time to be diplomatic or reserved—your career and livelihood are at stake!

It is also advantageous for you to seek guidance on performance standards from others in the organization. Surprisingly enough, your peers can prove to be especially helpful in coaching you to improved performance. You must remember that although the managers may have the power to hire and fire, they are not necessarily the best coach. Your peers may be able to provide insights.

Be careful with this strategy, though. As cold as it sounds, once you become "marked," more often than not, your fellow employees will distance themselves from you. They probably will not want to associate their careers with another that is on the skids. The other harsh reality is that despite the confidentiality of performance reports, forcing an employee out of an organization is highly political. Don't be surprised, if management, directly or indirectly, gives a heads-up to other employees about not associating with you. They may not want favored employees to tarnish their reputations—or they could be trying to isolate you in the hopes you'll do their work for them and resign.

If you have sought clarification from your manager and feedback from your peers and you still do not understand the required performance expectations, it may be time to seek additional guidance from the HR department or a second level of management. This strategy, however, does have its risks. Managers do not like their dirty laundry aired to the rest of the organization. Your intent should not be to complain about the supervisor or the process but to focus on obtaining clarity around performance standards. Specifically, this approach can accomplish the following:

- Reinforce your receptivity to the feedback and your desire to correct the performance problems
- Cultivate a more positive and supportive relationship with higher levels in the organization
- Provide the manager with improved coaching around communicating performance standards
- Just might save your job!

Even when you expect to successfully achieve the desired level of performance, it is important for you to realize that you might not actually achieve the goal. Understanding this reality, my advice to the professional is to update his or her resume, and start making phone calls. This is no time to be naïve. You will always be better served to hedge your bets to ensure continued employment.

Planning Your Exit Strategy

The other scenario, however, goes into play when you receive clear messages that the situation is going to lead to your departure or termination—no matter what performance issues are resolved. When a manager has lost all confidence, he or she can, and will, build any case desired to get a professional out of the organization. In this situation the best strategy is to actively manage your exit out of the organization. Beat them to the punch! It is absolutely possible for you as a professional to orchestrate the terms and conditions of your departure out of the company.

What most professionals do not realize is that when an organization looks to terminate an employee, they have a vested interest in ensuring that the process occur as smoothly as possible. Remember, companies are worried about reprisals from terminated employees. While nearly every state recognizes the concept of "employment at will" (wherein the employer can terminate an employee with no notice and for any nondiscriminatory reason), most corporate leaders hate lawsuits and do everything in their power to avoid them—so much so that their actions are often counterproductive to operating an efficient and productive organization. The key here is to capitalize on this concern.

Saving Face

When you can successfully facilitate your own departure from an organization and acquire a more substantive severance package, the transition into a new company may appear seamless to the rest of the organization. It is vital to understand, however, that negotiating the terms of one's own termination is a possibility that usually only exists for more senior staff positions in a corporation. In situations of potential termination, entry-level professionals have very little leverage to negotiate and are typically at the mercy of the organization. Before having any discussions about your exit strategy, consider the following issues.

1. *Do you really want to remain at work while you seek other employment?* While the old adage is true—"It's easier to find a job when you have a job"—today's business climate no longer attaches the same stigma to unemployment as it did ten years ago. This approach may assist the individual in keeping up appearances, but it can be difficult to show up every day to a company that no longer embraces you as a valued member.

2. *How much severance pay do you need to maintain your financial obligations while you look for a job?* While most corporations have general severance pay guidelines—typically based on position level and length of service—you might be surprised at the flexibility organizations often demonstrate in giving severance pay. One note of caution to the professional, however, is to be realistic. Corporations are not the state lottery. If your request is highly unrealistic, you may find that you have lost all leverage in the deal. After all, you are an employee who is going to be terminated. They are not predisposed to making you happy.

How Do I Do This?

Once you have clarity about the desired terms and conditions surrounding your departure from the company, the next step is to tell your manager that you would like to meet with him and a representative of the HR department. It is important to include the HR representative, as managers typically do not have the authority to make deals with employees.

Diligently rehearse exactly what you are going to say in the meeting. While such discussions are unfamiliar and quite unnerving to most professionals, it is important to remember that you are negotiating your livelihood.

The most important thing to remember is to communicate clearly and unequivocally. State that you have concluded that under the circumstances there will be no successful resolution to this problem and rather than going through the motions, you would prefer to orchestrate an exit strategy that accommodates the needs of all concerned. Explain what you are looking for in exchange for a quiet departure out of the organization. At this point the ball will be in their court.

It is important to understand that the company might not agree to your terms. On the other hand, the company may propose an alternative or compromised settlement. Either way, you are far better served by having proactively managed the situation than by waiting for the corporate ax to fall.

EXECUTIVE SUMMARY

Being on the receiving end of a performance improvement plan does not mean that your career is finished in an organization. Many employees have received performance coaching and disciplinary actions and successfully managed to achieve the desired performance results. However, you must be fully aware of the severity a performance improvement plan potentially holds for you—up to, and including, the termination of your position.

When faced with performance problems, your sole priority must be to correct the deficiencies and demonstrate an improved level of performance. Drive alone won't get you through—you must deliver the results. If you realize, despite your best efforts, that the outcome is going to be termination, make every attempt to engineer your own exit strategy. Many companies will provide some severance to preempt the risk of litigation—and to get you out of the organization. ◉

17 | TAKING STOCK: THE PROFESSIONAL ASSESSMENT PROCESS

N ow that you have a more complete understanding of the corporate dynamics, individual performance factors, and the critical behaviors necessary to achieve career success, the question then becomes, "What do I do now?"

I have designed a "professional assessment" plan to assist the working professional in better defining and implementing the necessary performance improvements in the workplace. These improvements relate to career choices and strategies, as well as specific areas of individual performance. The first steps of this process requires you to collect and analyze all the relevant corporate data and identify any cultural concerns that influence career success. Once you are clear on the corporate landscape, it is then time to collect feedback on your performance in an organization.

Business and Culture Assessment

The purpose of the business and culture assessment tool is to create a template with which a professional can begin to develop a more thorough understanding of critical business measures and environmental issues within the corporation. The attached outline will help guide you in identifying the specific drivers and culture of the organization.

Business and Culture Assessment Tool

PART ONE | KEY BUSINESS DRIVERS

- ◆ What makes the company money?
- ◆ What costs the company money?
- ◆ What is the long-term vision of the corporation?
- ◆ What are the company's key business strategies?
- ◆ How is the business performing?

ACTION STEPS REQUIRED
- ▶ Review the financial reports of the company—annual reports, 10-K, profit and loss statements, etc.
- ▶ Review the financial indicators for the corporation.
- ▶ Assess what is unclear about the financial performance of the business.
- ▶ Spend time with a representative of the investor relations group to discuss the specific drivers and financial indicators of the company.

- ◆ What functions directly impact the fiscal performance of the corporation?
- ◆ What is the primary role of each functional area of the business?
- ◆ Determine how functional strategies impact the company's overall performance.

ACTION STEPS REQUIRED

- ▶ Assess your current working knowledge as it relates to each functional area of the business.
- ▶ Identify the appropriate subject-matter expert. (Your manager can assist you in this process.)
- ▶ Schedule informational interviews with the select individuals.
- ▶ Prepare for the interviews—draft an outline of issues to discuss and the questions you have about the business.

PART THREE | CORPORATE CULTURE

- ◆ Does the culture value one's ideas?
- ◆ To what extent is the organization hierarchical?
- ◆ Does the culture promote cross-functional development?
- ◆ Does the environment promote open and honest communication?

ACTION STEPS REQUIRED

- ▶ Consider your own observations of the corporate culture and solicit additional insights from colleagues and superiors.

▶ Assess the alignment of the environment with your own belief system and professional objectives. Are they congruent?

▶ Determine your potential for long-term career success under the existing corporate culture.

PART FOUR | POLITICAL CLIMATE

- How political an environment is the corporation? My department? My supervisor? His boss?
- Am I overly influenced by my own personal agendas?
- Do I operate as a good steward of the corporation?

ACTION STEPS REQUIRED

▶ Consider your own observations of the environment and solicit additional insights from colleagues and superiors.

▶ Observe the behaviors of highly successful professionals.

▶ Assess the alignment of the environment to your own belief system and professional objectives. Are they congruent?

▶ Determine the potential for long-term career success under the existing corporate culture.

Performance Assessment Outline

As is discussed throughout this book, the most critical element in achieving a high level of success in the corporate world is the ability to deliver performance and value to a corporation.

The performance assessment outline summarizes many of the critical performance competencies, skills, and behaviors that contribute to the improvement of one's overall contribution and performance. You can use this tool in two significant ways: as a self-assessment tool and as a management feedback mechanism.

The first step requires that you honestly and candidly evaluate your performance in each of the specified areas. It is this critical eye that will lead you to a realistic self-assessment and to an identification of corrective strategies and approaches for improved performance.

This assessment will address personal career choices and strategies and then enable you to compare one's current career path to the insights gained from the business and culture assessment tool. This comparison will hopefully shed light on any misalignments between your career strategies and career paths most valued by the organization.

The final step is to use the assessment outline to guide discussions with your manager about specific performance issues and developmental efforts. The important point here is that management feedback should be solicited via discussions rather than yet another form to complete. The best strategy is to solicit feedback from your manager over several discussions, as the process can be quite time consuming. Lastly, you must reinforce your desire for open and honest feedback, and your manager should be made to understand that candor is key to the discussion—otherwise, what's the point of even convening these interactions?

PART ONE | SPECIALIST VERSUS GENERALIST

- The objective here is to assess your own current career direction and determine which approach is more highly valued by the organization.
- This assessment should lead to greater clarity around the direction of your career and potential changes in developmental opportunities.

CRITICAL QUESTIONS TO ASK

- ▶ Am I pursuing the career path I truly desire?
- ▶ Will my choice in career direction be rewarded and recognized by the corporation?
- ▶ Are those individuals being promoted specialists or generalists? Can both career strategies prove successful in this culture?
- ▶ Do opportunities exist for cross-functional and lateral moves?

PART TWO | CAREER POTENTIAL

- This assessment provides insight into your perceived career potential in an organization.
- The assessment will also provide critical feedback regarding longer-term career planning efforts and the overall investment the corporation is willing to make in your success.

CRITICAL QUESTIONS TO ASK

- ▶ Am I deemed as a high-potential employee in the department or division?

- ▶ Does the company employ a formalized success-planning process? If so, where do I fit relative to the department and discipline?
- ▶ Will my career be better served by investing in lateral moves to other areas of the company? Do I have the potential for those opportunities?

PART THREE | OVERALL PERFORMANCE

- ◆ This area of feedback addresses your overall performance and contribution to the department.
- ◆ You should seek further clarity on your perceived value to the organization and on the assessment of your ability to demonstrate a broader knowledge of the business and its drivers.

CRITICAL QUESTIONS TO ASK

- ▶ If the staff were force ranked, where would I fit? (See Chapter 12 for a description of force ranking.)
- ▶ Am I perceived as a top performer in the organization?
- ▶ What does your manager view as your greatest talents and strengths? What are the areas for improvement and your developmental opportunities?
- ▶ Does my performance reflect a broad knowledge of the business? In what areas do I fall short?

PART FOUR | PROFESSIONAL CURIOSITY

- ◆ This evaluation seeks insight and the evaluation of your ability to analyze, diagnose, and interpret problems and business issues.

- Specifically, you need to gain feedback on your approach to the job and your ability to evaluate issues in a broader business context.

CRITICAL QUESTIONS TO ASK

▶ Do I deliver comprehensive solutions and ideas when solving problems?
▶ Does my boss consider me to be highly curious and interested in the business, beyond my scope of responsibility?
▶ Are there ways in which I can improve my approach to solving problems?
▶ Am I doing what is required of the job, or have I changed the role?

PART FIVE | INDISPENSABILITY

- Analyzes your breadth of contribution and value to the organization.
- Seeks feedback on demonstrated performance as an expert in your area of responsibility.
- Further evaluates the significance of your position to the overall business operation.

CRITICAL QUESTIONS TO ASK

▶ Have I truly mastered my area of expertise?
▶ What short- and long-term developmental opportunities exist to strengthen that mastery?
▶ Do I fulfill a critical need or service that is unique to the organization?

► What are the areas of further exposure needed to broaden my overall knowledge of the business?

PART SIX | COMMITMENT/RESPONSIVENESS

◆ Seeks insight and feedback around your service orientation and the ability to deliver results on a timely basis.
◆ Further evaluates your personal value and integrity in meeting established commitments.

CRITICAL QUESTIONS TO ASK

► Have I established a reputation of reliability to my boss and the organization?
► Do I demonstrate a responsive attitude to all levels in the organization?
► Do I have a tendency to overcommit myself to projects and assignments?
► Am I meeting the needs of my boss?

PART SEVEN | COMMUNICATION SKILLS

◆ Addresses both verbal and written communication skills demonstrated in the workplace.
◆ Solicits feedback on personal communication style issues and your ability to actively listen.

CRITICAL QUESTIONS TO ASK

► Am I perceived as one who openly shares opinions and expresses ideas?

- ▶ Do I effectively manage conflict and promote an environment receptive to compromise?
- ▶ Do I actively listen to differing points of view and consider alternative approaches?
- ▶ Is my written communication effective and efficient to the organization?

PART EIGHT | CONSTRUCTIVE CRITICISM

- ◆ Provides a personal assessment of your receptivity to performance feedback, particularly constructive criticism and developmental needs.
- ◆ The process further assesses your active participation in soliciting performance feedback from superiors and colleagues.

CRITICAL QUESTIONS TO ASK

- ▶ Am I receptive to constructive criticism and performance feedback?
- ▶ Do I respect the opinions of my immediate supervisor?
- ▶ In performance discussions, do I demonstrate any defensive behaviors? If so, what are the observed behaviors?
- ▶ Do I actively solicit feedback about my performance?

18 | SUCCESS IS A SELF-FULFILLING PROPHECY

The most important truth to remember about corporate success is that there are no guarantees! For all of the advice and insight shared by these high-powered, influential leaders, the harsh reality is that even when you do everything right in the working world, you still may never reach the highest levels in a corporation.

Though this realism may sound a bit mercenary, the fact remains that factors beyond your control also play a pivotal role in the success equation. There is a lot of truth to the old adage, "Success is being in the right place at the right time." Even by their own admission, many of the executives described *luck* as a contributing factor to their career success.

The key for the highly driven, achievement-oriented professional is to cultivate a level of self-confidence that transcends the uncertainty of the working world. Success requires an internal strength and personal belief system that you can ultimately create your own destiny in the corporate world. As many of the executives described their journey to success in corporate America, each reinforced a genuine belief that if they functioned as a genuine steward for the corporation, operated with the utmost integrity, and performed at an exceptional level, the path to success would find its way to them.

It is this self-fulfilling prophecy that is perhaps the greatest lesson of all to the ambitious professional. Developing a self-concept that assumes preordained success essentially becomes the foundation from which true achievement can be attained.

Beyond a strong belief system and internal fortitude, the next step on the ladder of success is developing a level of expertise and competency that prepares you to capitalize on opportunities that present themselves. First and foremost, in each and every job assignment, you must commit to delivering exceptional performance. Regardless of the level or impact your position holds in an organization, your mindset must fuel a desire to differentiate your role from others in the organization and ultimately establish your own professional credibility and value to the corporation and its leaders.

As you have heard from many of the executives interviewed, tending to your interests must be balanced by a true desire to influence and drive a company's success. While these successful professionals indeed were achievement-driven, their primary goal was to attain a level in an organization whereby they could directly impact the strategic decisions and financial performance of a corporation. It was this objective, not personal agendas, that guided their commitment and conviction to maximize each and every job assignment.

Furthermore, each of these executives ultimately sought out industries, companies, and functional disciplines in which they had a genuine passion and curiosity. Here again, finding the most conducive environment will promote your desire to perform at an exemplary level and sustain the drive necessary to excel in today's demanding corporate arena.

True success is not about a paycheck, job title, or even stock options. It is about the indelible mark that you as a professional leave on a corporation (or several of them). My hope is that you find your way to success by serving a corporation, its shareholders, and employees with the utmost integrity and respect. Because when all is said and done, it is *who* you are, not *what* you have that is the truest measure of professional success. ⊙

INDEX